D1079282

PAID TO DECIDE

PAID TO DECIDE

*30 issues
no senior manager
can ignore*

JOHN FODEN

Business Books Limited

First published in 1991 by
Business Books Limited
An imprint of Random Century Limited
20 Vauxhall Bridge Road, London SW1V 2SA

Random Century Australia (Pty) Limited
20 Alfred Street, Milsons Point, Sydney
New South Wales 2061, Australia

Random Century New Zealand Limited
9–11 Rothwell Avenue, Albany, Glenfield
Auckland 10, New Zealand

Random Century South Africa (Pty) Limited
PO Box 337, Bergvlei, South Africa

Typeset in Baskerville by
𝐅 Tek Art Ltd, Addiscombe, Croydon, Surrey
Printed and bound in Great Britain by
Butler & Tanner Ltd, Frome, Somerset

British Library Cataloguing in Publication Data
A catalogue record for this book is available from the British Library

ISBN 0-09-174123-8

Acknowledgements

Many people have contributed to the making of this book. In particular I must thank Bill Williams, PA's Director of Corporate Communications, whose persistence brought it to birth. The midwives, it might be said, were Graham Jones and Andrew Osmond of The Company Writers, who helped us to put the words down on paper. My thanks to them too.

The book was much strengthened by the number of people inside PA who contributed ideas to it. Among those who helped were Thomas Ahrens, John Barbour, David Cook, Drew Dickson, John Ginarlis, Martyn Hobrough, Brian Houston, Graham Howarth, Michael Jackman, Neil Kilpatrick, Stephen Payne, Lars Procheus, Tom Sheridan, Paul Thornton, Donald Tilston and Glyn Tonge. Michael Thomas of Corporate Communications Strategy was also the source of many good suggestions.

This collective experience, culled from every discipline within the consultancy, is what gives me confidence in the book's authority. It does not rest simply on my own views.

However, the advice given here is my own. I take full responsibility for it and hope that it proves to be of some practical help to the men and women who are running businesses today. There is no group of citizens I admire more.

John Foden

Contents

		page
Acknowledgements		v
Foreword		ix

TOWARDS 2000

1	The challenge of the job	3
2	Into the nineties	6

UNDERSTANDING YOUR MARKET

3	Choosing your market	11
4	Excelling in your market	16
5	Extending your market	19
6	The quantum leap	23
7	The greening of business	26

MAKING THE MOST OF TECHNOLOGY

8	Technology: backing the right horse	31
9	Research: should you be doing it?	37
10	Managing research and development	41
11	Information technology: a matter for the chief executive?	45

DOING THINGS BETTER

12 Performance: the vital test   51
13 Good financial management: a fundamental tenet   58
14 Manufacturing: how to achieve break-out   65
15 Total quality: how do you get it?   70

MAKING THINGS HAPPEN

16 Strategy is making things happen   81
17 Mergers and acquisitions: are they taking us where we
   want to go?   88
18 Managing high growth   97

TAKING CARE OF YOUR IMAGE

19 Image and reality   107
20 Investor relations: to be loved, you must
   communicate   111

GETTING THE BEST OUT OF PEOPLE

21 The company atmosphere   121
22 Changing your company's culture   126
23 Building a winning team   130
24 The chairman and non-executive directors: a help
   or a hindrance?   134
25 Role and reward: don't be trapped by structure   140
26 Is the business suffering from demotivated
   managers?   142
27 Euromanagers: a new breed?   147
28 The art of smooth succession   150
29 Leadership is all   153

SUMMARY

30 A few rules for the road   159
   Index   162

Foreword

Chief executives, it will be argued, do not read books about how to be a chief executive. They don't have the time or the need. They're up there doing it already.

But no book has ever been written, or will be, that can tell a chief executive how to do his job. And this one is not going to try. All the busy CEO will find in these pages are a few tips and warnings, some common sense, encouragement and sympathy. And those are things he may be glad of, however busy. His can be a lonely position. My hope is that it will feel less lonely with this book beside him.

For simplicity's sake I've addressed it to one chief executive, standing for all, and I've made him a man, for which I ask the pardon of women in business. 'He or she', repeated every time it should be, becomes a tedious courtesy.

The book, I hope, will be of value to all those in senior management positions. Anybody who hopes to be a chief executive in the future, anybody who has to appoint one or is working close beside one right now, should understand what it feels like to occupy the desk at which the buck stops. The special responsibilities and priorities that go with the job are worth a bit of study by anyone with a serious interest in business.

The selective application of his energies, after all, is the mark of any good CEO. If he tries to do everything, frets about everything, he will not succeed in the job. But what, exactly, should he select? What ought to be the principal concerns of today's chief executive? On what should he focus his efforts as he leads his company towards the year 2000?

This book attempts to shed some light on the matter. It picks 30 issues for the CEO's attention and tries to say something useful on each.

My first qualification for writing it is that I have been responsible for a company for six years. So I know what it feels like. How hard it can be, and how rewarding. There are few problems mentioned in this book that I myself have not had to face at some point or other in my career.

Secondly, the nature of the work undertaken by PA Consulting Group brings me into frequent contact with other chief executives around the world. So I get to see and discuss how others do the job. This is how my working time is spent, now more than ever, and it gives me a useful vantage point.

The same is true of my colleagues, several of whom have made an input to these pages. Our job gives us an insight into what goes on in a CEO's mind. We are able to say with some confidence what worries him and what does not, what attracts his attention, what he tends to neglect, how he sees his own role and the challenges of the modern world. But to add a little rigour to the picture, we commissioned some research from the Corporate Intelligence Group. CIG's brief was to pinpoint the leadership skills required for corporate success in the 1990s. Chief executives of 27 large companies and banks, spread across all sectors of the UK economy, were questioned on their attitudes to markets, technology and finance. The resulting survey can only be regarded as a qualitative glimpse. Even so, it was interesting, and I'll be referring to it.

Although the survey was restricted to British-based companies, most of them have overseas interests, and this book will try to take a broadly international view. In putting it together I and my colleagues have drawn on examples from all round the world, as we were bound to do, because there are few businesses left that can afford national horizons. The modern chief executive, even if his company is quite small and specialised, is compelled to regard the world as one market. This can only be regarded as a good thing, but it does create new pressures and responsibilities, and I shall be taking a careful look at those. The job of CEO was never an easy one, but today it is more challenging than ever. If this book makes it any easier, even by a few degrees, it will have been justified.

John Foden
Chairman and Chief Executive
PA Consulting Group
London
April 1991

Towards 2000

· 1 ·

The Challenge of the Job

So you've made it. After years of climbing the corporate ladder – or perhaps through an early promotion, or perhaps by starting up your own company – you have become a chief executive.

And the odds are fairly good that somebody has already said to you, with a hint of malice mixed into their smile, 'I hope you enjoy it.'

'Thanks,' you probably answered, with a hint of foreboding mixed into your response.

And a little foreboding is in order. It is a hard job. Sometimes daunting, exhausting, confusing; often scary and always, to some degree, lonely. Don't take it on if your nerves are bad or you want to be loved.

This person who's ribbing you, for instance. Yesterday he was just a colleague. Today you're in charge and he's your subordinate. That's a big difference, and he must accept it, as you must. The top spot fell vacant; you stepped forward. That was your choice. You wanted the job and you took it, so you can't ask for sympathy when it gets hard.

Still, too much foreboding would be wrong. If your dominant feeling as you take the helm is one of anxiety, you're probably not the man to pilot the ship. Confidence, I'd say, is the one thing no chief executive can afford to be without.

You have to feel you can do the job. If you let it get you down, now or ever, you're in trouble. Nothing, indeed, should get you down: at least not for long, and not so that anyone would notice. Resilience is a prerequisite of leadership.

And how about a small swell of pride, a pause for self-congratulation, before your responsibilities close in? I think you could allow yourself that. In fact I believe very strongly that you should take pride in the job. Chief executives don't come ten a penny. They are rare and valuable people, who make the wheels turn for the general good. They are not, I think, valued by society as highly as they should be, and this is especially true in my own country, Britain.

At least it was true for many years. Now, in the 1990s, it is less true. Success in business is respected more than it used to be – though sometimes for the wrong reason. The creation of wealth, the cynic argues, is driven by personal self-interest, which should therefore be left to operate unshackled.

Anyone who meets as many senior executives as I do knows what nonsense this argument is. Material rewards are important of course, and companies must make a profit or die. But personal enrichment is not the goal which drives most people in business. They work to produce something other people want, something better than the competition, something in which they can take satisfaction. They work to add lustre to their company's name, to support their families, to give their own lives a sense of purpose. They are driven by a complex of motives, not simply self-interest – and this is especially true of chief executives. Ask why they are doing it and you'll get a variety of answers, but I've never heard one say 'For the money'. He is far more likely to mention a mission he hopes to accomplish, a vision he is striving to realise, than how much he is being paid to do it.

Yes, to head a business enterprise is an honourable calling, and you should take pride in it. It can also be tremendous fun. Let's not forget that. To you, as chief executive, the excitement of winning, the satisfaction of success, will be especially sweet.

And you won't be without support. Though you can't ask for sympathy, you can ask for help. If you're any good at all, you will create around you a team whose loyalty and camaraderie you can rely on, in bad times or good. They will strive to help you succeed, and one of your own chief pleasures will be to help them realise their own full potential. That's another mark of the true leader.

So it should be with confidence, pride and pleasure that you take up your new position. Your skin should be thick enough to take the knocks and your mind should be fixed on the challenges ahead. They are going to require all your energy.

· 2 ·

Into the Nineties

Our survey into the attitudes of UK chief executives showed a generally optimistic world view. Most of them agreed that, despite the usual dangers and difficulties, the 1990s were full of promise. Potentially, this could be a decade of progress and opportunity, despite its difficult start.

I find this attitude cheering, but is it typical of chief executives elsewhere? Broadly, yes, I think it is.

Certainly the other attitudes revealed in this sample can be found around the world – and that is not surprising. The globalisation of markets means that all are confronted with the same or similar business conditions. The CEO's role does not vary much from country to country, nor by type of business. Such differences as exist are usually related to the stage which a company has reached in its evolution.

Our sample did not feel that their role had changed much in recent years or was changing now. In their view the CEO had several clear responsibilities. It was his job to develop a strategic plan; to gather the right team around him; to communicate well, especially with the media and financial institutions; and to be the agent of change within his company.

What has changed, however, and is changing still, is the business environment in which these responsibilities have to be carried out. On this point a slightly more anxious note can be heard in the comments of the chief executives questioned.

Market boundaries are disappearing, they agreed. In more and more sectors, activity is becoming worldwide. This presents an opportunity, but also a threat. Competition can come from anywhere.

They were also much struck by the speed with which business is conducted today. The pace has increased dramatically, mainly because of increased competition and the impact of communication technology. This calls for rapid decision-taking, which in its turn is helped by the speed with which information can be processed and disseminated.

They agreed, too, that markets are becoming more polarised. To succeed, you either have to be very large or occupy a well-defined niche. Even if large, you have to choose your market segments carefully. Nobody can beat the world at everything.

And it is becoming more difficult for companies to succeed on their own. As markets expand geographically, joint ventures or other forms of cooperation are often the only way to take full advantage of the opportunities for international growth. The rising costs of research and the huge sums involved in technology are a worry, and this too is leading to more collaboration. The search for suitable partners or acquisitions has become a regular item on the CEO's agenda.

These were the trends revealed by our survey. Three others, I think, will mark the decade to come.

The first is the pace of technological change. We're all so familiar with this that it has become a cliché. Even so, it ought to be mentioned, because it is by no means a spent force. In the 1990s, I believe, we could see technological changes that will make the 70s and 80s look slow by comparison. Whole markets, whole industries, could be swept away and new ones created in their place.

A second point is that the thrust of innovative effort in industry is shifting from processes to products. In this the Japanese lead the way. In manufacturing methods they have long set the pace: here, perhaps, the scope for radical improvement is diminishing. But in radically new and better products they continue to astonish the world, and no doubt further wonders are to come. Other nations are only just edging out of their process revolution towards bigger, bolder product initiatives.

Thirdly, there is a growing consensus that clarity and boldness of vision are essential to corporate success. Strategies, spanning three years or so, need to be set within a vision that covers ten. The great success stories of modern industry – Japanese, European or American – all have this element in them of visionary purpose unswervingly pursued.

Industry will have to back its winners with more resolution than ever before, and to help it do so, the financial markets should be more willing to invest in long-range industrial plans. Governments, too, could do a lot towards encouraging the longer view. Besides improving education, training and the infrastructure – all necessary to long-term industrial success – they should think about providing a specific stimulus to technological development. Manufacturing industry is the essential engine of wealth creation: as such it deserves every possible encouragement from government, who must set the targets, point the way and create the right environment.

How can industrialists be expected to take the long view if financiers and politicians don't share the same horizon? The resolve to be industrially competitive must include every sector of society. Here in Europe, for example, we must learn to think of ourselves as a major industrial power, committed to long-term success within the world economy.

The modern chief executive, in short, must respect the necessity for long-range forward planning, and in this he can be greatly helped by a supportive social and economic culture. Without that support he will have a hard struggle.

Understanding Your Market

· 3 ·

Choosing Your Market

You may have reached the top spot through a marketing career. Some chief executives do. But that shouldn't tempt you into dashing round the world trying to prove you're the company's best salesman. Perhaps you are, but it's not your job. You have more important things to do.

Occasionally, however, it is important to place yourself visibly at the front of a sales effort. Sometimes you should take the lead in the search for business, because there are doors which only a chief executive can open; and sometimes you should come in towards the end. By demonstrating that it has your personal interest, you can help to close a deal well. But these interventions, and the time that you give to them, need to be chosen with care. Don't allow them to tickle your ego or fill your diary. Once you've made your contribution, go back to your office and carry on thinking. That's what you're paid to do – and it's harder than selling. 'Most people would rather die than think,' said Bertrand Russell. 'Most people do.'

Your job isn't marketing: it is to *think* about markets. But how should your thinking be organised? What are the priorities?

Our survey showed that chief executives spend more than half their time on market-related issues, but no clear consensus emerged as to what these consist of. Broadly, it was agreed, the CEO should concentrate on competitive strategy. 'How well are we doing? Could we do better? Are we aggressive enough?' These were the main worries. A general concern was expressed about the globalisation of markets and increasing competition, a general feeling that today you must either be very big indeed or occupy a well-defined market niche.

Watch out for that last idea, incidentally. Size and niche are not always alternatives. A narrow niche can be exploited globally – look at McDonald's – and sometimes it *has* to be, if it is to offer the return required.

In fact, if you think about it, all successful companies, even the biggest, occupy some sort of niche. They succeed because their products dominate a carefully chosen segment of the market. They are, as companies, *aimed* right.

And this is your first responsibility. You must be absolutely clear about which segment of the market your company's products are aimed at. Secondly, you must make sure that the total effort of the business is directed at that chosen segment.

Only you, the chief executive, can do this. Nobody else.

It's too critical a decision for the marketing director alone. He will spot opportunities, but is rarely prepared to accept the discipline of focus. He will have a point of view, he will have a contribution to make. But he cannot take the critical decision. Only you can do that, drawing on all the specialist inputs required to complete the strategic picture.

Only you can ensure that your company's product is aimed at the right market segment – and you'd better get it right. Because this is the heart of the matter. A business can only exist by having the product or service which its market requires. Get this wrong and you don't have a business at all.

Think of Horlicks. Originally launched towards the end of the nineteenth century as a dried food for infants, it had considerable early success. However, by the mid-1920s it was coming under pressure from competitors like Ovaltine. J.Walter Thompson were appointed advertising agents and came up with the idea of turning Horlicks into a bedtime drink. Full marks to the Horlicks board for backing that one!

Consider PA, my own company. The world's biggest market for management consultancy is the USA, but does that mean we can go rushing in there with exactly the same portfolio of services as we offer in Europe and Australia, presented and organised in the same way?

No, it does not, I can tell you from experience. We are now

well established in America, but only after some trial and error. We got some things wrong to start with and had to adjust our act sharply. In short, we misread the market.

I'll come back to PA's own experience in a moment, but first let's pause to consider the American market in general. This is a digression, I admit, but well warranted in the context of this chapter. So many firms need to get that market right. So many get it drastically wrong.

It is like no other in the world. On the surface it bears certain similarities to other national markets, but these can be deeply deceptive. The USA is littered with the skeletons of foreign companies who tried to do business as they had at home.

So in what ways is the US market unique? That question could fill a book on its own, but here are a few short answers:

- The sheer size of it invalidates at a stroke the assumptions of most new entrants, having no comparison elsewhere in the world.
- Partly as a consequence of size, it is highly segmented; a mosaic of niches; and the good players move very quickly between them. It's hard to know where to set up your stall.
- Freedom and variety of choice are so central to American society that the customers welcome, indeed demand, a much wider range of products than Europe, from TV channels to branded cereals. The competition is hot, and any good idea quickly imitated.
- American culture supports and protects the individual far more than other cultures do, especially the entrepreneur. Small companies proliferate like mushrooms, popping up overnight in every conceivable niche of the market.
- The US market is strangely parochial. The country has such immense natural resources that it doesn't have to worry much about other parts of the world.
- The people are open, approachable, candid. Meetings are easily fixed with Americans, because they enjoy them. But just because they're happy to talk about something doesn't mean they are ready to do it. Decisions can be hard to obtain.
- The government sector is more chauvinistic than any in Europe, even France. To make a sale in the public domain is uphill work for non-Americans.

- America is not a national market at all, in the sense that most of us know, but an accumulation of localities, each with its own subculture. Styles of doing business will vary greatly between, say, Chicago, Los Angeles and Houston.
- Employees demand more of their employer, not simply in salary and benefits, but in all the fringe factors that contribute to the comfort, prestige and lifestyle of the job. They are also at liberty to leave on the spot. Mobility is higher . . .

And so on. The list could be extended, but this one is now long enough to demonstrate my point. The American market is like no other, and some of its features present special problems for the foreign company. Small wonder that so many fail. British Telecom has had its difficulties, and so has Apricot, rumoured in the press to have spent £14 million to achieve sales of £1 million in a single year. But it's possible to get America right, as Grand Metropolitan has shown.

To return to PA: we have made mistakes too. Some of the lessons we have learned may be helpful to others.

We assumed the market would be the same as in any other developed, sophisticated country. The majority of our managers were British and the business was structured in the way we were used to. We attempted to run a coast-to-coast operation from a single location and assumed that our reputation in the rest of the world preceded us.

If you visit us today, you will find some important changes. Firstly, we have spent a lot of time and money analysing the consulting market in the United States, selecting the skills that differentiate us in that market, and deciding what had to be done to make those skills attractive to potential clients. We discovered that it was necessary to apply a degree of rigour to the analysis unparalled elsewhere.

We found two keys to success: focus and culture.

Focus is applied by geography (we concentrated on the East Coast) and by industry (we concentrated on no more than three or four sectors) and by service (we concentrated on skills that are technologically oriented).

Even so, our chosen market niche is so large that we haven't bumped against its edges.

Culture is critical. We have grown to understand the consequences of a society that accords unusual respect to the rights of the individual. We have learned to cope with the wider but shallower career experience of our employees, and the higher mobility that is a consequence of this. Above all, we have learned to change as fast as the market does – faster than anywhere else in the world. That has meant liberating the business from European structures and attitudes. It has also meant fewer British managers. Most of ours are now US citizens.

Don't worry, at no other point in this book do I talk at such length about my own company! But our shaky start in this most difficult of markets seemed to me an experience worth sharing.

The moral?

Choosing your company's market is not a simple matter, even though it's a vital one. In the end the decision can only be yours, but many different disciplines can be called on to help you get it right.

Focus is essential. You must choose markets where you can win today and expect to win tomorrow, and your business may need to be more tightly defined overseas than it is at home.

The one sure error is to leave such decisions to your marketing people. Remember the two shoe salesmen who were sent out to a new market many years ago? One cables back: NO MARKET HERE – LOCALS GO BAREFOOT, and the other: NO SHOES HERE – GREAT MARKET OPPORTUNITY.

Which telegram would you have torn up?

· 4 ·

Excelling in Your Market

Having chosen your market, you must strive to excel in it. The two requirements are almost one. If you've aimed it well, your product is likely to succeed; if it fails, you probably got the market wrong.

But there is a shade of difference here, and in it lies your second big marketing responsibility. Having picked your segment, you must prevail. First you must choose, and then you must win.

So how will that be achieved?

We talk of the need for our companies to be 'market-oriented', 'market-led'. But nowadays that is too passive. Everyone is led by the market, as everyone piously repeats. The clichés of business slip off our tongues. We probably mumble them in our sleep.

In the 90s something sharper is needed. Let's call it *market focus*. Success, I believe, will only go to those companies which are entirely focused, from top to bottom, on providing some unique value to the customer. There must be some edge to their product which none of their competitors can match. And retaining, increasing that edge – it can easily be lost – must be an obsession which grips the whole company and continually drives it forward.

True market focus is a very rare thing. I would guess that only one or two per cent of companies have succeeded, really succeeded, in creating a culture of that sort. And again it can only come from the top. Only you, the chief executive, can bring it about. But it is a hard, hard thing to do. No magic exists. Only vision and leadership and drive can create a company whose total effort is focused on keeping a lead in its market.

The trouble is, nothing stands still. Today's unique edge is commonplace tomorrow, and old hat the day after that. So the vital dynamic that has to be instilled is a ceaseless, energetic quest for new and better ways to provide extra value to the customer.

Continuous product improvement, continuous anticipation of demand, are a matter of course in such companies – and the very acme of success is a wholly new product which meets a need no one saw before.

Think of the British and American markets for mineral water. Who would have guessed they were there until Perrier found them? The company saw an opportunity to exploit the move away from alcoholic drinks dictated by a growing health-consciousness. And the high price of the product was a help: it became smarter, in an era of conspicuous consumption, to be seen sipping a Perrier than a gin and tonic.

Think of cling film, think of photocopiers and fax machines. Think of cellular phones and cassette recorders. How did we ever live without them?

Such innovations are not created and kept alive by advertising. They succeed and endure because they fill a real need. In the end people buy what they want, not what someone tells them they ought to have. The best new products are discovered by thinking hard about actual, everyday human situations and how they might be eased or improved.

The idea for cat's eyes can only have come from thinking about the way drivers follow the curves of the road by night, peering forward for reflected objects beyond the immediate range of their headlights. More recently, an imaginative innovator gave some hard thought to the predicament of the DIY enthusiast whose home is too small for a workbench. Result, the Workmate, developed so successfully by Black & Decker.

Good new products, in short, only come from a company which is completely focused on the market. Only by being exactly adjusted to the latest requirements of the customer will you succeed. Any loss of that focus, any slackening of the effort to maintain it, will quickly lead to serious trouble.

Consider, for example, the recent competition in small computers. Amstrad's plan was to enter a high-priced market with a low-cost product; its edge consisted in a combination of cheap manufacture and good marketing. Apple launched its PC without a clear market in mind, but it caught on in offices, being rather expensive for the home. IBM then elbowed it out of the market with a more sophisticated machine, designed specifically for office use, so it switched direction and went for desktop publishing with the Apple Mackintosh. That's a good example of winning by rapid adjustment – unlike Sinclair, who rested too long on his early success. Every home wanted a Sinclair, then suddenly it seemed too much like a toy, and the market left it behind.

In the market-focused company the one unforgivable sin is to get caught napping by the competition, and it doesn't only happen in the sudden-death world of computers. Consider tennis. Slazenger and Dunlop, resting on years of market leadership, failed to foresee the demand for bigger racquets. Prince was able to steal a march. Nor does competition always come from recognised competitors. Yamaha has been making musical instruments since 1887; only in 1955 did it break into motorbikes.

To prevail in your chosen market sector, you have to keep up with the latest technology, certainly. But the one and only benchmark of success, the thing you must never take your eyes off, is added value for the customer. That is what you have to provide, and it doesn't always come from technical wizardry. Concorde, for instance, is an outstanding technical achievement, but too few customers value the saving in time sufficiently to pay the price. Consider, too, the Betamax video cassette. Technically, this product of Sony's was better than the VHS, but that is no help if the movies which the customers want to see are only available on VHS.

So market focus comes first, and every bright technical idea that lands on your desk must be subordinate to that. If it doesn't bring some extra value to your customers, some lead against your competitors, then it is irrelevant and should be discarded.

Goodness knows, the game is hard enough without distraction. Keep your company's eye on the ball!

· 5 ·

Extending Your Market

So you pick your product sector and strive to be the best in it: all well and good. But markets are not like football fields, neatly marked out with white lines that never change. Product sectors shrink or grow larger, blur into others, sometimes vanish altogether. They can be altered by technology, competition, social change or simply the swing of fashion.

So it's essential to keep an eye on the boundaries. Are there other markets you could be selling your product in? Are there other products you could be selling in your market? Are you making full use of your brand?

There is a natural momentum which will lead you, very properly, to develop your existing product as far as you can and introduce new ones that are closely related. To concentrate too narrowly for too long would make you vulnerable to change.

A key role for the CEO is to know when to focus exclusively on winning in existing markets, and when to be pushing out the boundaries and developing new ones. Whilst incremental development can normally be accommodated, and should be encouraged, anything which adds to management stretch should be carefully reviewed.

And remember, there is a right time and a wrong time for developing new markets. Coloroll, for example, in its headlong rush to conquer new markets, forgot how to make money in its old ones – with disastrous results.

The second aspect of the CEO's role in developing new markets is to understand whether a proposed diversification is playing to the company's strengths or not. At some point it can be said that a company is stepping off its patch, and it's his job to recognise where the patch ends.

Some diversifications are recognised as gambles from the start. They are either going to sweep the market or die. Sinclair's electric car comes to mind: doubly risky, because it combined diversification with what was seen as a radical market innovation. (In this case death might have been predicted, since the product came nowhere near fitting its niche.)

In other cases the risks are less obvious. On the surface, a diversification can look like a logical extension of your existing activity, but that is where you have to be especially careful. Beware of false similarities.

It is easy to see how Saatchi was led into management consultancy. It looked like a natural add-on to its marketing services. In fact it is a totally different business, run by different people with a different approach, different skills, different disciplines; and although the target client base was the same, Saatchi had underestimated the resistance to cross-selling. The company had in fact entered a different market, and one it didn't understand, but given its immense resources it made a bigger mistake of it than others might have. It paid too much for a plethora of companies that had little in common.

Nothing, however, can match the initial havoc caused by diversification in the City of London. As deregulation removed the walls between financial services, the scope for error was magnified. Banks became stockbrokers, and insurance companies turned their hands to estate agency, in many cases with little success, and sometimes with catastrophic results.

Some of the early diversifications, such as Lloyds Bank's entry into estate agency or Security Pacific's link with Hoare Govett, were achieved through a sensibly priced acquisition and formed part of a well-considered strategy. Then an element of fashion came into the picture at the general expense of reason. Encouraged by the bull market of the mid-80s, a feverish me-too scramble began as the big financial institutions chased a limited number of stockbrokers and estate agencies. Hasty purchases were made, at reckless prices, and some of the resulting mergers turned out to be painful mismatches.

False similarities are the trap – I'll mention this again when I come to mergers and acquisitions – and the best illustration of it was the purchase of estate agents.

At first glance, the logic was sound. In making these acquisitions, the banks, insurance companies and building societies were trying to protect their access to the market. They were afraid that estate agents, being so strong on the ground, would start selling financial products. The customer's primary need was a house, after all; loans, life policies and mortgages were merely means to that end. Vertical integration, from the customer back to the supplier of finance, seemed to be a smart competitive move.

The problem was, for the institutions, that they didn't understand the dynamics of the market. Estate agencies are dependent on volume, and if it goes down you can quickly make a loss. There was also a failure to understand the differences in the customer's perception of an estate agent and, for instance, a building society. Estate agents are regarded as salesmen; their job is to move houses. A building society is not like that. It is a professional guardian of your money. Its image is traditional, and desirably so. In the customers' eyes the two types of business are utterly different: one is frankly commercial, the other an ethical service.

Small wonder that some of these marriages went wrong.

One very simple moral can be drawn from this. A diversification of any sort must always be the outcome of your long-term corporate strategy; it should be carefully planned, and implemented without haste or pressure. If it is hurried, opportunistic, defensive or imitative, beware of it. Fashion is not a good yardstick in business, and although much has been made of the stimulative effect of mergers and acquisitions on the stock market and the economy, their effect on the companies concerned is dubious. There is a mounting body of evidence to show that the company taken over, even unwillingly, often gains more from the inflation of its share price than the victorious predator, who has to foot the bill.

What rule can we draw, then, from these mistakes? If you hear the word 'synergy', be ready to run? No, there are times when diversification makes sense. The key to success is to have a clear idea of how the synergies are going to be realised, and this is an art I'll be discussing in Chapter 17, which deals with mergers and acquisitions.

This chapter has put more stress on the ways in which diversification can go wrong; and in these we can now observe a pattern. A dangerous diversification is one which takes you wholly off your patch. To succeed, you must understand the market, or the product, or the production process – any one of those three; or, better, two of them. If all three are new to you, you're compounding the risk. You will probably fail and take the whole business with you.

Don't do it – and shoot down the sillier fantasies before they even get raised in the boardroom. Diversification excites people, especially those who've grown bored with their jobs. As chief executive you must be quick to restrain such emotions, which have no place in planning a business.

· 6 ·

The Quantum Leap

There are moments when being a chief executive requires just plain courage and determination. Some risks can't be ducked or delegated. Only you can take the decision, and in doing so you place your head on the block.

I can think of several examples, but probably the ultimate test of nerve is the long-range development of a new product.

Your existing product has been improved and improved, keeping pace with every advance in the technology on which it is based. But these incremental improvements are subject to diminishing returns. They cost you more and more, they bring you less and less. The lead that they give you is slight and soon lost, because the competition is so quick to follow suit.

So what do you do? Do you stay in the race or do you make a quantum leap, switching to a new product based on totally different technology?

In any good company – any company which is fully responsive to change – such dilemmas arise from time to time. They don't occur often, and perhaps you won't have to face one during your own period in office. However, if you do, you will need strong nerves.

A classic case is Pilkington's switch to float glass. At enormous cost the company developed a radically different process of glass manufacture. It was more cost-efficient, produced glass with better optical qualities and, incidentally, was more environment-friendly, since the 25 per cent of the thickness of the glass which had to be ground off under the old process was washed away as an unpleasant slurry. The development of float glass took seven years and cost many millions of pounds: a great act of faith on the part of the company's directors. It paid off, and now Pilkington licenses the process to the world. But would the City have supported such a gamble? That we'll never know, because Pilkington was a private company at the time.

This was an extreme case of *process* development: a new way was found to make the same thing. Once the process was mastered, the market was known. An investment was made to reduce the costs of manufacture, and that was a risk which could be quantified, even if in Pilkington's case the early arithmetic was rubbished by technical snags.

In *product* development the risk is greater still, because the market, too, is unknown. You are making something new, something never seen before, and the price is dictated by the cost. Will people buy it or won't they? Will a competitor beat you to the draw with a similar or better product? You won't really know until the product is launched, by which time your company's life, not to mention your own position, may well be hanging on the answer.

In the field of venturesome products there is no case history to beat the Sony Walkman. Would people want to walk around with earphones attached to their heads? Sony's marketing people said no. They did not even bother with market research, convinced they knew they would get the same answer. Nonetheless the chief executive backed his own hunch and said yes, let's do it. The launch cost is reputed to have been $5,000, spent on handing out a few free samples to the trendiest people in Tokyo with the suggestion that they roller-skate round the city wearing them. The rest is history.

In some cases, product and process risk are meshed together. A change of process can be so radical that it changes the product significantly. One could argue that this was true of Pilkington, where quality was so much improved that it led to new applications of sheet glass. But I'm thinking more of the service sector, where a good example is Midland Bank's launch of First Direct, the branchless bank. I'm thinking about the competition between the petrol companies to offer better service at their filling stations: a good case of incremental improvements with diminishing returns. Which company will be bold enough to scrap the old system completely and design an automated fill-up where the driver (as in the good old days) does not have to leave his car?

No account of new product risk would be complete without a respectful mention of the pharmaceutical companies, who live with it all the time. Millions are spent, years of effort are put in, before a new drug can be brought to market. And here the big risk – perhaps the ultimate risk in commerce – is that there will be no product to show at the end. The market potential of a cure for diabetes or migraine is predictably large, and drugs like Zantac, Glaxo's treatment for ulcers, have been hugely success-ful; but this has to be set against the awful possibility that the line of research you are following is a blind alley, or that unforeseen side-effects will turn a potential winner into a disaster, as in the case of Opren.

In none of these cases, I should add, are we talking about a total shot in the dark. The pure, outright, win-or-die gamble has no place in business. There is always some information to hand – forecasts, market research, cost assessments, expert technical opinion – which will bring an element of rational calculation to the decision. Through pilot projects and test marketing, much can be done to manage the risk, and if yours is a business that is routinely faced with such decisions you are likely to have a portfolio of high-risk and low-risk opportunities.

However, from time to time decisions do have to be taken on which the future of the company depends, and these fall squarely on you, the chief executive. At the end of the day you will have to back your own judgement – and there's nothing wrong with that: you're paid to have it. But you should as far as possible try to ensure that the high-risk decisions you take are in areas you do indeed understand, where your antennae function, where your nose twitches. Retail banks, for instance, can afford to make adventurous decisions about retail banking products, but not about obscure overseas markets.

A quantum leap, by definition, requires some courage. But it should never be totally a leap in the dark.

· 7 ·

The Greening of Business

When the supertanker, *Exxon Valdez*, ran aground in Alaska, even the world's biggest oil company could not ignore the voice of environmental concern. Under pressure from institutional investors, Exxon announced it was appointing an environmentalist to the board to advise on future company policy.

Until quite recently the green lobby had little impact outside West Germany and a few other European countries where the issue had become political. But now concern is much wider. Bhopal, Chernobyl, the *Exxon Valdez*, the greenhouse effect, toxic dumping, the destruction of rain forests, the massacre of whales and a host of other man-made events have forced environmental issues onto the corporate agenda.

At a recent PA dinner, most of the companies who attended said that care for the environment now figured prominently in their strategic thinking. And if this is not true of your own company, you should give the matter some thought. Your personal views on the issue are irrelevant. Environmental pressure is a fact of life, and the companies who succeed in the future will be the ones that recognise that fact and respond accordingly.

Remember, too, that there are genuine business opportunities in meeting environmental concerns. Anita Roddick built the Body Shop on an environmental platform. She did it by producing environmentally safe cosmetics that haven't been tested on animals, by selling them in re-usable bottles and by packaging them in bags made from recycled paper. She has let the whole world know what she is doing and has used each shop as a forum for educating the public about environmental issues. She was also smart enough to be slightly ahead of the trend, but not too far ahead, so that by the time green became respectable, her brand was well established.

ICI has had to face the fact that people, worried about the earth's atmosphere, are increasingly reluctant to use chlorofluorocarbons (CFCs). It has discerned, however, that the needs of the market have not diminished; rather they have changed, and into areas where the Group's technology can really make a difference. From being just a commodity supplier of CFCs, it is now one of very few companies in the world to be offering a CFC-substitute.

The more the constraints close in, the greater the opportunity to differentiate yourself from your competitors, and the greater the prize.

The important thing to bear in mind about the environment issue is that it represents a *change in the market* – a change in customer preference. This preference reveals itself not only in what the customer will or will not buy, but in legislation. The law, after all, is merely a reflection of the will of the consumer.

A change in legislation, in other words, is only another reflection of a change in consumer demand – and that is the right way for business to look at it.

Consistency has little to do with it. The will of the people, as often, is hypocritical. In America there is legislation requiring cars to be fitted with catalytic convertors, but what would be the public reaction if the government tried to reduce pollution by putting a $2 tax on a gallon of gas?

The green issue, like all other market factors, is a series of mutually exclusive trade-offs. Ask people what they want in airline travel, and they will say lots of leg-room, four seats across a 747, great food and low fares. But they cannot have all of these things. One perhaps, or two; not all. Likewise with the environment.

Green business is just the same as any other sort: a matter of reconciling contradictory consumer preferences. Success comes from close social observation, resulting in a product with the right mix of trade-offs. However, this must be done seriously, not just as a short-term ploy. Customers are quick to rumble the companies that merely stick a green label on existing products.

Environmental concern is not just a passing fad, and the market-sensitive company should be constantly gauging the future. What will be the next change in the law, the new pattern of social behaviour? And how can the business take advantage of these patterns, developing new products that address tomorrow's consumer tastes and lifestyles?

The answers are never easy, but in every really good businessperson there is always a dash of pure foresight.

Making the Most of Technology

· 8 ·

Technology: Backing the Right Horse

There was a time when all the best watches came from Switzerland. Then came electronic technology from the Far East, and suddenly the Swiss watch industry was in trouble. Cogs and flywheels, however beautifully engineered, were no match for quartz that could do the job more cheaply to an accuracy of a few seconds a year. Although the Swiss retaliated well with the Swatch, they had been comprehensively outflanked.

Anyone whose product or process contains a technological component must feel a pang of sympathy. No-one is immune to the surprise innovation that renders a business – sometimes an entire industry – obsolete overnight. And if anything, the danger is greater now than it was then.

Technology continues to change at an ever greater speed. It has been calculated that Sony alone brings 3,000 new products to the market every year, each one a technological improvement on its predecessor.

At the same time, products and processes are incorporating an ever greater *range* of technologies. A car, for example, used to be a piece of mechanical engineering. Now it could well incorporate electronics, optics, catalytic chemistry. And just when you're getting to grips with those, along come airbags, which embrace a whole family of technologies. Suddenly the car manufacturer needs to know about sensors, propellants and detonating systems.

Technology is also becoming global. Today's big corporations regard the whole world as their field of operation, acquiring their technology *wherever* it happens to emerge and exploiting it wherever there is a market. So threats are no longer local, they're international: as the Swiss discovered, a company's product or process can be overtaken by developments taking place literally anywhere in the world.

Like it or not, we're in a technological spiral. To stay ahead in the market, you've got to keep adding to, or changing, your technology base. Added to which, technology has its own impetus: you can't stop scientists inventing things. The markets are pulling, technology is pushing, and the cycle of change is accelerating.

Our research shows that most chief executives are aware of the problem but don't know how to respond to it. Which is hardly surprising. How many chief executives understand monoclonal antibodies, micromechanics or neural networks, any of which might be just the breakthrough they need – or a dangerously expensive red herring?

If you don't understand the technology, how can you evaluate the opportunities or threats it poses? How do you know if your R&D is heading in the right direction? What do you do if you're already invested to the hilt and suddenly the technology steps up a gear? Is it worth even *trying* to keep up? Those were typical worries unearthed by our research. At least one of our respondents dreaded hearing of new developments for all the extra trouble they might cause him.

This uncertainty in the face of fast-changing technologies is reflected in the often ad-hoc way that companies go about their research. Funding levels are decided more on the basis of what a company can afford or what it spent last year than on any commercial criteria. What we often see is a mixture of faith and scientific method: 'If we give those research chaps a million, maybe they'll come up with something useful. Or then again, they might not.'

Many companies dither between pouring money into R&D – in the hope that the rainbow's end is just over the horizon – and reining in costs even at the risk of killing off potentially useful projects.

All in all, it's the stop-start, rule-of-thumb approach that all too often prevails in the funding and management of R&D – which is not good enough, given the risk of falling behind if you get it wrong and the market opportunity if you get it right. You must choose the technologies you need to invest in and manage them in a way that puts you ahead of the competition. No other course is open to you.

It's complicated, but it need not be *that* complicated. The skill, if you choose to compete, is to link your technology to what you're trying to do in the market.

Sometimes technology-push can overthrow one line of research and institute another, but the impetus can just as easily be market-pull – in fact it more often is. Johnson & Johnson, for example, would never have considered tamper-proof packaging to be an important technology had someone not put poison in its Tylenol. Suddenly the market demanded tamper-proof packaging and Johnson & Johnson, to its credit, was one of the first to crack the technology. Their success in this lifted the sales of Tylenol to a new high.

In creating your technology portfolio, it's essential to balance the pull and the push. It's no good developing a technology for which there is no market application; but there's no point, either, in keeping abreast of your market if you don't have the technological resources to meet its needs when you see an opportunity.

Research and marketing can no longer be kept in watertight boxes. They have to be seen as opposite ends of the same activity.

Such issues are by no means restricted to the big corporations. A year or two back, Keeler, a small British manufacturer of medical equipment, identified a market need for a new type of tonometer – the machine that measures the pressure in the eyeball and so helps to diagnose glaucoma. The existing products were heavy bench machines and you virtually had to clamp the patient's head before you could use them. Nobody liked them, but nobody had thought of anything better. With help from PA, Keeler came up with a neat, hand-held tonometer that you simply point at the patient's eye. The machine itself senses when it's properly aligned, activates itself automatically and produces the result on a digital read-out. It has subsequently outstripped the competition.

The point is, you don't need enormous R&D resources in order to contemplate a new technology. Technologies are available; and if you can't afford to develop them yourself, you can always buy them in.

But there's still the question of deciding which technologies to invest in. How can you be sure that the horse you're backing won't be overtaken, or simply fall over, before the last fence?

This is difficult. There are plenty of examples of expensive research programmes which came to grief because somebody else got to the market first or came up with a better idea. However, I would argue strongly that if you know your market, your choice of technology in many cases decides itself.

An acquaintance of mine makes plastic bottles. He makes them for antifreeze, he makes them for pesticides, but he hasn't made many for beer. That's because the carbon dioxide in beer migrates through the plastic and shortens the shelf-life. He's solved the problem by coating the inside of the bottles with a very fine layer of material that's impermeable to carbon dioxide. He's now opened up an enormous new market for his product. And if I were a manufacturer of glass beer bottles, I'd make sure I knew what the plastics men were up to and take steps to protect my market.

So you're not operating blind. If you know where you are on the business map, and you know where you want to get to, it's not so difficult in many cases to decide which technology to ride. It's if you *don't* know where you're going that the problems arise and confusion sets in.

All that I've said so far presupposes that you, the chief executive, know which technologies are available and whether or not they might be useful. In Britain, the chief executive is statistically unlikely to be a technologist and in all probability doesn't know one end of a microchip from another. And why indeed should he?

To chief executives who don't know about technology I would simply say, find yourself someone who does. Give *him* the responsibility of monitoring relevant technologies and alerting the board whenever he identifies either a threat or an opportunity.

It may sound obvious, but it's surprising how many company boards, certainly in Britain, expect to absorb technology by some form of osmosis or by what they watched on television last night. The Japanese, in contrast, are very clear about who supplies the technological input. 'It is him,' they will say, and mention a name. 'That person tells us about technology.' PA's research shows that 80 per cent of Japanese companies have such a person on the board, as against 20 per cent in Britain.

Your task as chief executive is to ask that man the right questions. 'Do I need to be worrying about biotechnology? Can it help us improve our product? Is the market interested in it? Have our competitors got onto it yet?' And so on. The important thing is that these are *business* questions, quite capable of being asked by someone with no technical expertise at all.

It follows that your technical director should not be just a boffin, but market-aware as well. I was always impressed by the fact that Beecham never appointed anyone as head of a research unit until he had done three years in a market-related job. Your technical man may know all there is to know about gene-splicing, but unless he has a feel for your markets he cannot give you the business answers you need.

It's also important that this individual should not be under pressure to defend his R&D budget or argue the case for any particular technology. If the success of your company depends on a switch from adhesives technology to skin chemistry, you'll never do it if the scientists on the payroll are fervent sticky-plaster men. They must be free of vested interest in any one technology if commercial imperatives are to prevail.

Technology is no more complicated than marketing, and it should be treated in the same way, i.e. by having someone on the board who knows about it. For the chief executive, the technology problem is not a *technology* problem at all – rather one of recruitment. The key is to choose with enormous care the man who will be your eyes and ears in the technological world – and then, quite simply, to ask him the right questions.

To that I would add one small but important rider.

In a high-spending area such as this, there are obvious dangers in appointing to the board a man whose expertise is so far out of sight that nobody round the table knows enough to challenge his opinions. One way to avoid this is to appoint a non-executive director with the same expertise, on whom you can rely for a second, impartial, longer-distance view. The balance of debate is then restored.

· 9 ·

Research: Should You Be Doing it?

Once you've decided which technology to invest in, you need to decide how to acquire it. Do you develop it yourself, buy it in wholesale, or go for a half-way option such as collaboration?

There are no standard answers – simply certain things to consider before you reach your own decision.

Let's first be clear about what's at stake. If your business is manufacture, there can be enormous advantages in incorporating some form of proprietary technology – a technique, a material, a capability – that is unlike anyone else's and that distances your product or process from that of the competition.

But you need to decide what price you're prepared to pay. If you develop the technology yourself, you get the kudos and the chance to make some money before your competitors catch up, but you also shoulder the entire cost and all the risk. If you co-operate with other people, you can share the risk and the cost but by definition you must also share the benefit. If you simply buy it in, you're spared the risk but you may end up making a me-too product by a me-too process.

In choosing your route, it's important to know the kind of company you are and therefore how much proprietary technology is appropriate. To help you decide (if you don't already know), let me suggest three levels of technological involvement, each of which calls for a different attitude to research.

The first and bottom level is characterised by a Sinclair or an Amstrad. Companies operating here are picking up other people's components and sub-assemblies, putting them together in boxes and branding and selling them. Some do it ahead of the pack, like Sinclair; others such as Amstrad prefer to follow when the product can perhaps be made more reliably. Either course is valid. But whichever you choose, the last thing you want to be doing is undertaking new development for yourself. Your aim is to squeeze out costs wherever you can, and that means letting other people do the difficult technological bits.

That's not to say you shouldn't be proprietorial about other parts of your operation. After all, nobody makes money in business unless they can do *something* that other people cannot. Your distinctive skill may be knowing the right suppliers, having a super-fast distribution system or offering a lifetime guarantee with each product. It can in fact reside in *any* of your activities as a manufacturer, and at level one it's often to do with service or logistics rather than with the product itself.

The important thing is to know what your distinctive skill is. If it's producing television sets in a particular shade of blue that nobody else can offer, that's the field to invest in. Get as good as you can at it and keep what you know to yourself. As for the rest, buy it in or do it in-house, it doesn't really matter.

There's nothing new in all of this. Defining and exploiting a distinctive skill is only what every village craftsman did in centuries past. The difference is that the fast-moving international market of today makes defining that key competence a lot more difficult. The answer may be far from obvious, particularly if you're right up close to your business and don't have a view of what's happening in the world around.

So for level-one companies, proprietorial technology is probably not an issue, though they do need something, somewhere, that's unique to them or they won't stay in business for long.

Level-two companies are those which turn research quickly and efficiently into products that the market will buy. Whether the research itself has been carried out by single companies or in collaboration does not particularly matter. The level-two company must simply know where to get its hands on the technologies most appropriate to its needs. Its interest is not in fundamental research so much as taking research that already exists and putting it together in innovative ways to meet market need.

After all, there was no fundamental breakthrough in the

compact disc player. (There was, perhaps, in the technology needed to manufacture the disc, but that's another story.) For the player itself, all the component technologies had already been developed, and the skill lay in putting them together to produce a system that worked. That meant, among other things, varying the speed at which the disc rotated so that as the pick-up moved towards the centre, the rate at which the signals passed the head remained constant. That hadn't been necessary with gramophone records, but now it was. The answer was not *new* technology, but the clever application of well-tried control technology to read the speed of rotation and slow it down accordingly.

At the third level are companies who *do* depend for their survival on fundamental research. Drug companies are an obvious example, because all they're really selling is a compound and they stand or fall by how much better or different is the compound they offer. But also involved at this level are companies researching new materials, new electro-optic devices or certain aspects of biotechnology.

It's unlikely, I think, that any of these will readily collaborate in fundamental research. They'll certainly do so further down the line (many drug companies allow their products to be distributed by competitors) and they may just do so if one partner makes cars and the other aeroplanes and they happen to share an interest in a particular technology. But in so far as fundamental research is the key to their success, they'll keep it to themselves as far as they possibly can.

In reality, however, only the big battalions can *afford* to do very much fundamental research. It's a high-expenditure, high-risk activity, and economics, if nothing else, are forcing more and more companies to do it collaboratively. If governments reduce their commitment to support fundamental research in universities and academic institutes, then industry must take the strain. So more cost and more collaboration.

Our own research in Europe and Japan shows that about 40 per cent of large manufacturing companies have undertaken collaborative R&D. And most who have would claim to have benefited from it.

The choice is yours. Decide where your key competence lies. If it's somewhere in the technological realm, decide to what degree it needs to be yours uniquely. That decision will in turn determine how you acquire it – on your own or in collaboration with other people.

And a final thought. I've concentrated here on research – either alone or in collaboration – as a route to acquiring new technologies. It's by no means the only one. If you've identified a technology you need and somebody else has it, it's often cheaper to buy the company.

· 10 ·

Managing Research and Development

In the last two chapters we've looked at how you select the technologies you need to be good at, and whether your technology should be yours and no-one else's. Sometimes it should; sometimes not.

Let us suppose now that you've defined an area that your company is going to research. How do you get best value from the exercise?

Well, money obviously comes into it. The more you put in, the more benefit you'll get out – or so one would assume. But that's not entirely the case. PA recently asked 400 chief executives in Japan and four European countries how satisfied they were with the results of their R&D. The results show an interesting disparity between expenditure and value gained. The high spenders were not always the most satisfied.

The key ingredient, more important than mere money, is how well your R&D is *managed*.

In broad terms, managing R&D means integrating the activity into the company's overall strategy in a way that many Western companies have so far failed to do but which the Japanese are very good at. The process is two-way. Corporate strategy must take account of the possibilities inherent in today's technology. Conversely, all activity on the technological front must be guided by strategic considerations. In short, it is no longer possible for the strategists and technologists to sit in separate boxes. Their skills must be dovetailed.

So what does this mean in practice?

The first thing to do is separate the 'R' from the 'D' – the research from the development. This is crucial, yet surprising numbers of companies continue to lump them together and refer to 'R&D' as a more or less single activity. They *must* be seen as different.

I would further suggest that each is itself divisible into two distinct types or phases, thus producing a four-point spectrum. To reduce it to very simple definitions:

- *Pure research*, largely done at universities, investigates the nature of things and how they work.
- *Applied research*, largely done in industry, takes things as they are and tries putting them together in new combinations to create new effects, which are demonstrated in a prototype.
- *Development* goes on to refine the prototype into a product which can be sold on the market.
- *Product maintenance* finds ways to improve an existing commercial product.

It's always a valuable exercise to take your own R&D and dissect it into these four boxes. The important question then arises: how much are you spending on each, and have you got the balance right?

Few companies will get deep into pure research, unless of course it's critical to success, as it is in the pharmaceutical industry. Most companies, however, commit some resources to applied research, and even more will be involved in some sort of development. Product maintenance is a necessity for everyone: without it you're hardly a serious player. But the danger to watch for is that you're spending *too much* in this fourth box. If most of your R&D budget is taken up by product maintenance, then you're not really breaking new ground and you're likely to wake up one morning to find you've been overtaken. You'd be in the position of a car manufacturer who was putting all his effort into better magnetos and braking systems without ever actually developing a new model.

Choosing what position to adopt on this four-point spectrum is a crucially important part of running a business today. Periodically you must take a long look at your product range and assess what mix of R&D it depends on. Are you being left behind by the market – or are you possibly getting too far *ahead* of the market? Either mistake can be expensive. The skill is to define the line and then choose your best spot along it.

So given that 'R' and 'D' are different, with different contributions to make to the company's success, how should they each be managed?

Research has the longer time-scale. It needs a style of management that sets the strategic direction but doesn't rule out the accidental discovery or the pursuit of promising sidelines. Development, on the other hand, is tight-track. By definition, it has to meet a specific market need at a specific time. That requires a very different style of management.

Managing research

Having chosen where to concentrate, and set the direction for the company's research effort, the board must then create the conditions that will make it productive. It needs to find a balance between central control that avoids inefficiencies and duplication, and a level of autonomy that gives researchers room to exercise their own initiative.

Increasingly, given the premium on quality research, a technology-dependent company must offer conditions that will attract the best people. Surprisingly, perhaps, large salaries are not the most important consideration. Recent studies by PA have shown other factors to be higher on most researchers' lists, such as the freedom to exercise their own judgement; open debate; good contacts with outside bodies; and a minimum of interference from non-technical managers.

If this menu of incentives would put an intolerable strain on your company, perhaps you should think again. Better not to do research at all than attempt it with second-rate people.

Managing development

Once a company has built up a technological portfolio that fits the needs of its market, it must then pay close attention to the way it manages development. The transition from a technology to a successful product can be handled well or badly, and corporate success depends more and more on doing it well.

The key, once again, is integration. Successful companies tend to be those that have broken down the inter-functional divisions. There needs to be free flow of information between research, development, design, manufacturing, marketing and all the other functions along the route from concept to launch. The marketeers need to communicate market demands back through the process to R&D. Researchers, in turn, should be market-led, directing their efforts at known and quantified market needs. The entire effort needs a single director and a project team that can pull together the necessary resources from end to end of the company.

A well-managed development process will achieve a number of things. It will shorten the development and implementation cycle for new products and businesses, ensuring faster response to competitive threat and market opportunity. It will speed the integration of new technologies, whether they be applied to products or processes. It will ensure, finally, that the product is relevant to the company's business and right for the company.

In conclusion, the globalisation of technology and the rate at which it is now changing are going to lead in the future to even shorter product life-cycles. The companies that survive will be those than can access technology from around the world and quickly turn it into new products appropriate to their markets.

As we saw in the previous chapter, collaboration is one way of going about it. But the key, in my view, is the *management* of R&D – distinguishing between the two activities and controlling each in a way that yields maximum commercial benefit. The better companies perform in this area, the more successful they are likely to be.

· 11 ·

Information Technology: A Matter for the Chief Executive?

There are few subjects on which CEOs differ so widely as the extent to which they should become personally involved in information technology. Some see IT as providing technical solutions to technical problems, which can safely be left to the IT or DP manager. Others see IT as central to their business strategy, a means of differentiating their products and services from those of the competition, and they like to get personally involved. Perhaps the most commonly held feeling is one of reluctant but compulsory involvement. The sheer size of the decisions – many hundreds of millions of pounds, in the case of banks with their retail networks – demands the attention of the CEO, however ill equipped he may feel to intervene in this area.

The problem is compounded by the astonishing pace of change. It is only 20 years since order-processing was thought to be too complicated an application for the computer, yet who today would do it by hand? Ten years ago the idea that the average executive car would have up to a dozen microprocessors in it would have been thought fantastic.

Moreover, advice is poured on the chief executive from a staggering range of sources. Computer manufacturers have attracted the world's top marketing and sales personnel, the press is full of it, and IT consultancy is an industry in its own right.

So how much do you need to know – and do?

In the first place you need to have a balanced attitude to the whole topic. Hostility to IT has no place in the boardroom, but reckless enthusiasm can be just as dangerous. Companies have been bankrupted by the all-singing, all-dancing, integrated solution to their requirements. Such projects consume vast sums of money yet can easily fail to deliver the benefits promised.

IT can do a lot for most businesses, and will soon be able to do a great deal more, but it does need to be properly directed. There are, I think, five key areas which require the intervention of the CEO.

Firstly, you must ensure the user gets into the driving seat and remains in it. Whilst IT specialists are needed to draw your attention to the opportunities available, the decision about which applications are worthwhile must be made by the line managers. Many companies such as ICI are now addressing this by appointing an IT director who has experience of marketing, production or general management. The trend is for users, or ex-users, to become the managers of major IT projects, and this is to be welcomed.

The second thing to make sure of is that your company has the right IT architecture. Your basic computing and communications requirements must be properly met by your major systems. This is a field in which casual decisions at an early stage can force you down paths which cost a great deal of money and frustration later on. The decision to buy one supplier's local area network may constrain the PCs you can buy, or the software packages you can run, in ways you didn't expect. This is one area where a second opinion should always be sought.

Thirdly, time is of the essence, and you should beware of the over-engineered solution delivered several years down the line. In general, provided your basic architecture is right, you should insist that new applications are delivered rapidly, even if that means accepting a lower standard of engineering. It may be better for half your users to get onto the system next quarter than all of them in two years – and here is where packages can help. Your IT specialists will tell you they won't save money, and they're right; but packages will save you time, and this may be the most valuable commodity.

Make sure, fourthly, that you are getting all the mileage you can out of your existing software. Very often an initial application is capable of being extended to meet a wide range of further requirements – not perfectly, but adequately. So don't let the best oust the good. Clarks Shoes provide a good example. The company is in a business where speed of response is all – or nearly all. The year's fashions are unveiled at one or other of the major fairs, after which shoe production becomes a race. The manufacturer who is first to deliver the new styles to market has a crucial head-start on the competition. Clarks quickly realised that computer-aided design would not only speed the initial drawings, but could almost instantly turn the basic design into a score or more of different fittings. The next bottleneck was making the cutting tools for each model of shoe. Clarks decided that the same information that produced the drawings could also make the tools, and so on, down the line. Today a single set of data controls practically everything, from drawing to finished product, and Clarks shoes are in the shops remarkably quickly.

Finally, when you are faced with a major systems development, make sure you manage the *benefits* as well as the implementation of the system itself. Take the clearing banks, with their billion-pound IT investments. Several of them have developed database systems, at great cost, which enable them to target customers for particular products. The purpose, of course, is to cross-sell the products of the bank, but are they managing the benefits of this? Have they researched the willingness of customers to cross-*buy*? Have they trained their staff to handle the selling role? Have they invested in their products to make them easier to cross-sell?

In IT, these are the five priorities. The specialists are getting much better at building systems that do what they're supposed to, on time and on budget, but as CEO you must ensure that any expenditure is directed towards valid business aims and doesn't take on a life of its own.

Doing Things Better

· 12 ·

Performance: The Vital Test

Performance has overtaken and enveloped productivity as a measurement of company success. The change is a good one. Productivity, a more limited notion, carries with it a whiff of the sweatshop: greedy old capital squeezing more output from poor old labour, against resistance from the unions.

In a modern industrial economy this picture of factory life is increasingly out of date. Productivity improvements are more likely to come from the workers themselves, organised into small units and allowed to suggest any changes they like.

At Fuji Xerox, for instance, management recognised that they needed to double labour productivity over a period of two to three years. They did this with the help of hundreds of thousands of suggestions for improvement put forward by their own employees. So great was the desire to cooperate that ideas were popping up at a rate of over one per employee per working day.

This story, though it bears the inimitable stamp of Japan, is typical of modern productivity improvements. It shows what can be done when individuals begin to think about their jobs differently. Many similar examples could be drawn from other companies. But to say that such methods are universal practice would be an exaggeration. They can only succeed if responsibility for productivity, as well as the authority to make changes, is pushed down the line to the people actually doing the work – and not every company is willing to do that. It can only be a matter of time, however, before such procedures become the accepted norm.

In a recent survey conducted by PA with the help of the CBI, most companies claimed they made some effort to measure productivity, but many of them only did so on the factory floor. This makes no sense at all. The use of energy, materials or assets can be measured for productivity, as can information technology and every sales or office function. There's nothing difficult about it, and yet our survey showed that in British companies about half the staff received no regular information on the results achieved by their own department. This can only mean that no measurement is occurring, or the staff aren't being told about it. Either way, the lapse should be put right.

It's this limited view of productivity that is causing the term to slide out of fashion. Performance is a better word, because it represents the current notion that every activity of the company can and should be measured for results.

Technology has contributed to the change. Productivity, in the old sense of output per man, has less importance now that automation has reduced direct labour to a smaller proportion – typically, 15 per cent – of the manufacturing cost base. It is less likely to concern you as CEO than it would have in the 1970s, though if you run a service business, particularly in the financial sector, you may have to pay it more attention. Labour productivity in a dealing room full of expensive young talent can be of profound concern to the chief executive of an investment bank or securities house.

Performance, on the other hand is bound to concern you, whatever your company does. Operational performance, quite simply, is the difference between success and failure. To ignore it would be as peculiar as saying that you didn't care about your company's results.

So here is another item for the chief executive's personal checklist, and it breaks down into four questions which you should always insist on asking:

- How do we *measure* our performance?
- What are the root *causes* of our performance?
- What are we doing to *improve* performance?
- Is there general *commitment* to these improvements?

Those are the questions which have to be asked. And if, to any of them, there is no answer, you're in trouble. Quick steps should be taken to find the answer and act upon it.

Let's take a closer look at each question in turn.

Measurement

Measurement is the precondition of action. You can't improve your company's performance until you know what it is – and the only way to know is to measure it. There are several kinds of measurement that can be used, sometimes in combination with each other.

The first, and most obvious, is to compare your own company's performance against the best for your industry. Most industries do have some published comparative data, and some industries – finance, automotive, airlines – are almost swamped with such information. Using it to draw accurate conclusions is never easy, but the effort is worthwhile. There is always some indication of performance to be had here.

Functional standards can be useful too. In any industry there are always some rules of thumb: the usual size of a personnel department, the usual stockturn, the usual maintenance spend or marketing budget. If your own company is out of line with such norms, you should pause to give the discrepancy some thought. What's the reason? Is it a good reason?

The year-on-year trends within your own business are a further source of guidance. Performance can't be judged by a snapshot; it has to be looked at over time. Human nature dictates that the upward, impressive graphs will find a place on the wall where everyone can admire them. They may even be pinned up behind your desk, as in the standard cartoon. Poor indicators, on the other hand, tend to vanish in the filing system where they can disturb no-one. Trends which compare badly with those of other companies can easily be glossed over or rationalised; some special factor is discovered which invalidates the comparison, and everyone leaves the meeting reassured. But you, the CEO, should have a special fondness for the awkard question. 'Why *are* our widgets selling less well in Asia? Why *really*? Is it, as John says, a slump in the Pacific? Or are the Koreans just making better widgets? And if they are, how long will it be before they break into Europe?'

There is a trend in bad trends. At first they're ignored, and then they're acknowledged to be 'mildly worrying' and then they become an 'investment we needed to make', and finally they're a crisis. It's your job, as CEO, to put the spotlight on them early. Otherwise the crisis will be yours.

Analysis

But the quest for knowledge doesn't end there. Next comes the harder step of understanding *why* your company performs as it does. This is a more analytical, qualitative type of investigation – but every bit as important. Until you understand the root causes of your company's performance, how can you set about improving it?

Again, you don't have to grope in the dark. There are some useful, well-tried procedures to hand which will lead you to the answers you need.

The first step is to think hard about the basis of competition in your industry. Is it all about cost, or is there something else, more important, which sorts the winners from the losers? Is it product quality? Speed of delivery? After-sales service? Find the answer, and you'll be well on the way to understanding your company's performance. Perhaps you are strong in some ways but weak where it really matters.

Secondly, take a hard look at your measures of success. How do you decide if you're winning or not? Is it just a question of the bottom line, or are there other important indicators of performance? Market share? Unit cost? Delivery times? Your share price and p/e ratio? Companies develop certain habits in this regard, certain indices which everyone automatically watches. Question them! In measuring your company's success you can't afford to be bound by habit or the clichés of business thinking.

You must dig deeper if you want your action to be effective. What levers should you pull to bring about what improvements? The answers can only be found by identifying what really drives your performance, what really drives up shareholder and customer value.

The surface will only tell you so much. What might be called the visible performance of your company may well be presented to you in traditional form. You know your profit, you know your share price; you can see your sales levels and market share; and here are your costs, laid out, as usual, by department or type of activity – fixed costs, labour costs, costs of materials. All this is standard, and will lead to standard decisions. 'If we cut material costs by A, we can expect a profit improvement of B.' It's relatively easy to look at a normal set of accounts and arrive at such conclusions. But are the real drivers of performance hidden under the figures, obscured in some way by the standard analysis of costs and revenue?

The only way to know – and it's always worth doing – is to take an *oblique* look through the organisation, asking questions the ordinary figures may not have answered. 'What's our product profitability? What's the profitability of each market sector? How do our customers regard us? Are we losing orders? Are our good people leaving, and if so, why?

No-one will thank you for it, but asking awkward questions is an important part of a chief executive's job.

For example, a company can be failing because it's trying to do too much. The cause of its poor performance is nothing more than dilution of management control. Excessive diversification has led to such complexity in its reporting systems that no-one can tell any longer where it is or is not making money. Many successful turn-arounds have begun with the stripping out of irrelevant activities.

Another potential red herring, especially in service companies, is the cost of their infrastructure. Perhaps the important question is 'Do we need this infrastructure at all?' As this book goes to press, it is still a little early to say whether First Direct, the branchless bank, has transformed the UK banking industry. Nonetheless, win or lose, this bold initiative is a good illustration of what can happen when somebody dares to ask some new questions. Why *do* banks need premises in every high street? What is it their customers really want from them, and are there simpler ways to provide it?

Such questions defeat the standard indicators. But they need to be answered. If you haven't analysed your distribution cost or your product profitability, you're likely to be overtaken by a more sharp-witted competitor.

Improvement

The improvement of performance is rarely achieved by a single step. Programmes of action, with different time-horizons, are the usual thing. Often a whole family of initiatives is required, in the short term, medium and long.

In the short term, the priority is likely to be operational efficiency. This requires constant attention, and sometimes, if survival is at stake, you will have to take drastic action. But take care, when cutting away the fat, not to damage too much of the muscle, or you'll find it hard to resume your strategic course once the crisis is over.

In the medium term, the emphasis is likely to be on improvement of policy and technology. Now you'll have time to review the organisation, its development and the people within it. Is it too complex? Can it be streamlined and simplified? Are there too many layers? Would a flatter structure, with shorter chains of command, be more efficient? Can the organisation be changed and the people developed to serve better what the business is trying to *achieve*?

That last is the crucial question, and it isn't often approached with the thoroughness it deserves. In the marriage of organisation to business, some startling mismatches can occur.

Take NHS hospitals, which used to have a strongly bipartite structure. On the one hand were the clinical staff committed to providing the best possible care for their patients; on the other were the administrative staff striving for cost-efficiency. Inevitably there was conflict. With two such separate priorities, the organisation tended to pull itself apart rather than pull together towards a well-run hospital. At least here the problem was recognised, and the clinical staff have now been given more responsibility for cost-efficiency.

In the long term, improving performance depends on your corporate culture. That's where the commitment comes in.

Commitment

It's a relatively simple matter to obtain commitment to a single improvement programme, especially when survival is at stake.

The real challenge is to create a corporate culture in which continuous, self-renewing improvements are automatically generated. Such commitment isn't easily achieved. Elsewhere in this book I take a longer look at the dynamics of corporate culture, but here I'll just mention that the final stage of raising performance must be to make the process *stick*.

Among the initiatives required will be attitude-changing and quality management programmes. Improvements should be seen as a continuous process. To some extent this can be achieved by putting in the right controls, but the ultimate test of success is a culture in which people don't need pushing. They volunteer ideas and take action on their own from a natural, instinctive desire for improvement.

Such collective dedication is rare outside Japan. But it can be achieved, and it has to start with you. As chief executive you must be committed to raising your company's performance, because it is the test of your own. You won't be able to do everything yourself, but you must have a clear overview of the various initiatives and keep on driving them forward.

And never, for a moment, stop watching the results. Vision has its place in what you can do for your company, but here it's your hard nose that's wanted, your ability to keep up the pressure. Better performance must translate into better results, not necessarily overnight, but at some stage. Otherwise it counts for little.

· 13 ·

Good Financial Management: A Fundamental Tenet

It is terribly easy to put too much into a book of this sort. 'To be a good chief executive, you must do this and this and this . . .' The author who covers every inch of the ground is covering his back against criticism, but he won't have offered much practical advice. In the end all he's saying is 'Get every bit of it right and you'll be good at the job.'

That's why I'm sticking to the 30-odd things that seem to me to present the most important claims on a CEO's attention. It's a selective list, which reflects my own experience and opinions. Within it, however, there are one or two items of indisputable importance. They might be defined as those responsibilities which, if neglected by the CEO, will bring disaster on his head. One such is financial management.

Survey after survey has shown that by far the most frequent cause of business failure is lack of adequate financial control. As this book goes to press, in the spring of 1991, some very big names are in trouble. This is true internationally – there are whispers about some American and Japanese banks – but even more evident in the UK, where punitive interest rates and falling sales have stretched many companies' resources to the limit. Some of the fast-growing stars of the 1980s are fighting for their lives. The empire of Rupert Murdoch is pressed for cash. Polly Peck has just passed into administration, and the tall poppies in Australia have been cut.

Hard times put a sudden harsh spotlight on the need for strong financial control, but without it even the good times will not be as good as they should be.

At one level there is a simple answer to this. Get yourself a good finance director.

But what *makes* a good FD? That's not so easy to say. The exact place he fills in your team is worth some careful thought, because his role is multi-faceted, with different facets applicable to different companies.

In every company the role can be divided into external and internal responsibilities. Externally, your finance director will be the channel for discussions with bankers, auditors and lawyers, with brokers and analysts – if the company is listed – and with government agencies. He must deal with the Inland Revenue and exchange control authorities. It's his business to see that statutory reporting requirements are met.

Internally, he must ensure that the business is soundly administered and adequately financed. Although it's not his job to see that you make the right product or sell it well, he must understand the business and be capable of identifying the key information that will help you to manage it profitably.

The best finance directors will also make the corporate funds work for the company. Through good cash management, they can make a substantial contribution to the company's profitability.

If he is a qualified accountant – in my view, this is essential – your FD will be a member of a professional institution. Although he is employed by the company and owes it his loyalty, he is also subject to the rules and regulations of his own professional body, which he must obey in preparing your company accounts. What may seem a trivial issue to you can be quite troublesome to him. He has to tread a narrow line, and this should always be borne in mind. Ignore it and you won't get a good man in the post.

In the best companies the finance director is an important figure, whose close collaboration with the CEO is always central to the firm's success. Indeed chief executives often take their FDs with them when they move from company to company, or even from division to division within the same group.

So this bilateral relationship – as important, almost, as that with your chairman – should be created with the utmost care; and the balance of it will vary from case to case, depending on your own level of competence. Clearly if you are a gung-ho, blue-sky entrepreneur with plenty of drive but a limited understanding of numbers, you'd be wise to put a good solid accountant at your side. If on the other hand you have an accountancy training, you may think you can do the job yourself. But that is always a mistake. As CEO you will have many other calls on your energies, and the finance job is far too important to be handled on the side. Lords Weinstock and Hanson, though they have financial training, don't try to be their own finance directors.

Chief executives come in all shapes and sizes, and so, it should be noted, do finance directors. Some are experts in taxation, some are masters of cash management and the hedging techniques of international treasury; some are used to working in small private companies, others have experience of the pressures imposed by quotation on the stock market; some have an intimate knowledge of financial institutions and the City; some have a gift for forward planning, others are specialists in financial engineering.

What is your main current need? Good cash control? Good systems? Each company will have its own priorities, depending on the nature of the business and the state of its development. In addition, each chief executive will have his own requirements, depending on his own mix of skills and the balance he wants to achieve in the board. Together these factors will determine the sort of finance director you need. Analyse them well and choose him with care, always bearing in mind that you may need a different type of FD in a few years' time.

Balance is the key. The best proof of that, I'd say – at the risk of sounding unduly pessimistic – is to look at some of the things that can go wrong when the balance is lost. An over-powerful finance director, for instance, will tend to arrogate areas to himself that he knows nothing about. His control of capital expenditure, combined with a negative attitude, can throttle a company. If the divisions have to jump whenever the FD pulls the strings, this can raise a whole host of antagonisms.

Excessive bureaucracy in financial reporting is another danger: the dreaded monthly packs and the massive reporting of detail. This can happen all too easily. The FD should see that the monthly reports to the board provide them with the information they need to manage the business – no more, and no less. Apart from the obvious items, he must ensure that the key drivers of the business are identified. In relatively few companies, I'd say, are such monthly packs provided and properly analysed. More often the reporting requirements are in place, but the information remains unused at head office; or else it is automatically passed to the board, to whom it is of no interest, because it obscures the information which is fundamental to running the business.

An omnipotent CEO, free to overrule his FD, is another unbalancing factor, which can create serious trouble for the company. The figures provided for public consumption must be true and fair, and those for internal consumption must accurately reflect the trading position. Many of the cases that have recently hit the headlines were triggered by a lapse of this sort.

In large multi-business groups a problem can arise when divisional accountants adjust the figures they send to head office because of their awe of the divisional chief executive. The group FD must make it quite clear that any such manipulation of divisional results is a capital offence. There is always some latitude in the way results are presented, but this must be confined to the corporate finance function, and the view taken must be conservative, never optimistic.

The ability to forecast is essential to successful management, and the truly valuable FD will spend a large proportion of his time forecasting. Beware of the 'Gentleman Comptroller', who produces a fine set of backward-looking accounts, correct to the last penny but at the same time deeply misleading. He probably has a marvellous relationship with his auditors, but the company, meanwhile, is being driven on its rear mirror. The subsequent crash can be sudden and terminal.

Back in the 1970s, PA was advising Court Lines, a charter airline, on a question of organisation. At one point in the assignment our financial consultant was sent in to do some work on the figures. On the day he arrived, the board was lunching the Mayor of Benidorm and had just appointed a Head of Corporate Planning. The atmosphere was calm and confident. But after a few hours with the accounts, our financial man went straight to the head of the PA team and reported that here was a client in serious trouble. A few days later the company was bankrupt.

In all these cases of failure some element of balance has been lost. The critical factor in good financial management is a carefully balanced relationship between the FD and CEO, adjusted to their personal strengths and the needs of the company. Obviously, tight control and accurate information – including forecasts – come first; but over and above these two necessities there are critical areas of decision in which you can profit from the skills and advice of a good financial man.

It is financial management we're talking about, note, not accounting systems. But obviously the two interact, to their detriment or benefit. So a word about systems is in place here.

Agáin, the key is balance. There are two excesses to avoid: too much flexibility, and too little.

No system should be so spongy that people can manipulate it for their own ends. It is all too easy for figures to become weapons in the tussle for personal advantage. If you've come up the corporate ladder yourself, you'll be familiar with the games people play.

There's the wildly optimistic forecast to compensate for a lacklustre year. There's the budget deliberately padded out in the expectation of being cut back to the figure desired. There's the manager who tries to charge costs away from his division to appear more profitable than the others. There's the trick of distracting the board from larger issues by a single small item of dubious arithmetic, or the contrary tactic of drowning the issues in a deluge of accurate but superfluous fact. Computer output, expressed in incomprehensible jargon which nobody dares to challenge, is perhaps the favourite trick of all.

A good FD will have none of such dodges. He'll kill them at source and protect you from any half-truths, whether concocted through fear or ambition. The people at the centre of the company must be able to trust the figures produced by the various divisions or business units, who can't be allowed to keep any tricks up their sleeves.

In a big multinational, especially, such games have disastrous consequences. But a good FD will forestall them by establishing his own independent network. The finance man of each business unit, though reporting to his managing director, should also have a direct line to the chief financial officer of the group. This liaison can be strengthened by FD's conferences, in which they are all periodically called together. Shell has done this for many years.

So much for the dangers of pliancy; but perhaps more common is the accounting system that exceeds in rigidity. You want something new, different or bigger and your accounts department says sadly, 'It can't be done; there's no way we can account for it'. I've seen companies miss the big opportunity because it was either impossible or too much trouble to put together the necessary budget. All the money was already battened down and there was no way it could be prised out from the various pots to which it had been assigned. The strategy was stifled by the system.

But no accounting system should *control* anything. All it should do is provide information so that the people in charge can exercise control in the best interests of the business. The system is there to serve the company's strategy, not vice versa.

In this respect the FD's role is similar to that of the technical director. It is no good his baffling or obstructing the board with specialist knowledge. He should be capable of interpreting financial matters in terms his colleagues can understand. His job is to ensure that business decisions don't make financial nonsense, and vice versa. To do this, he must appreciate what the company wants to achieve and be able to shape the accounting systems to serve those objectives, not frustrate them.

Budgeting, I've noticed, is especially prone to rigidity. All too easily people start to treat budgets as fact. Just because the figures add up, they assume that is what will happen next year. The danger then is that they don't react fast enough when events take a different turn. A budget is built around forecasts and targets; the moment those assumptions have been invalidated – for better or worse – you can start to lose control of your costs, because you've moved so far from your point of origin that you no longer have a meaningful way to measure what you're actually spending against what you ought to be spending. Answer: scrap and re-set the assumptions, make a new plan and set a new budget, however much work is involved.

Such quickness-on-the-feet is vital in modern business. Flexibility, I'd say – in all matters except the accuracy of the figures

– is the single most important characteristic of a good finance director.

Take a company expanding off its national base into Europe. How does it measure, assess and present the totality of its performance? Each step of the way its accounting systems are likely to undergo changes, some of them rapid and radical. Perhaps Europe should be treated as one big pot, with each national subsidiary responsible for revenue in its territory but profits assessed on a pan-European basis. Or perhaps the system should work by business sectors that cut across the European territories.

Whatever financial structures existed in the past, the company must be able to change them as circumstances alter. If it can't, or doesn't, the accounting conventions will start to put a drag on the strategy.

With today's information technology, it is not too difficult to create a database that can be looked at from any angle. If the system is flexible enough, you'll be able to ask it, 'What were last year's costs in Germany? What was the revenue in Europe in January? How much profit did we make in the banking sector in the third quarter?' The data can be cut any way you like, depending on what you need to know. If this kind of flexibility is built into the system, it will save you having to re-analyse your figures every time your strategic priorities change.

So think through the kind of flexibility your business needs, discuss it with your finance director, and get him to create a system that serves the company's objectives.

It is this sort of close, intelligent, strategic double-act that you should aim for with your FD. Nothing less is good enough.

· 14 ·

Manufacturing: How to Achieve Break-out

For decades, manufacturing companies have tended to think of performance as something to be improved by gradual stages: 'This year we'll try to raise productivity by three per cent, and if we don't succeed we might try again next year.'

That sort of approach might have worked in the past but it won't any more. The world is such that you can't stay competitive just by turning up the 'better' button. You need to think far more in terms of 'break-out'; of the step change that puts you dramatically ahead of the game.

Several routes are open to you. Three of them – Total Quality, technological innovation and information technology – have chapters of their own elsewhere in the book. Here I want to concentrate on a fourth. This is *rapid response*: knowing what your customers want and so organising your manufacturing and distribution that you get it into their hands faster than your competitors.

As so often, the Japanese provide a model.

The car manufacturer, Toyota, recognised early on that winning in the car game meant offering variety. But going for variety meant it couldn't make for stock, it had to produce to order. Allowing so many days for delivery, the company realised that to stay competitive it had to complete each car within two days of receiving the order.

One of the keys to success was how quickly it could change the press tools. Toyota looked at what other people were doing and discovered that Volkswagen could effect the changeover from left

to right hand doors in four hours. (Other European manufacturers at the time were taking 12 to 16 hours.) Soon Toyota,
too, had got down to four hours. But that was still not good
enough, so the management decreed that door presses needed to
be changed in 12 minutes. The immediate reaction from Toyota's
engineers was that this was impossible. But they did it.

The story holds at least two important lessons for other
manufacturers looking for break-out.

The first is that change of this sort will only happen if the
impetus comes from the top. If management has decided that
the company cannot succeed unless door presses are changed in
12 minutes, it must stick to its guns. It must also face the
possibility that anything and everything may need to be done
differently.

The reason most car companies couldn't change their door
presses in less than half a day wasn't that they weren't clever
enough; rather that they'd fallen victim to ingrained thinking.
Setting up door presses had come to be regarded as a black
art that only the initiated could undertake. All Toyota did
was replace black art with simple science, solving the problem
with some intricate but not particularly exotic production
engineering.

So management must apply the pressure, at the same time
being open to the possibility that absolutely everything may need
to change.

The second moral of the tale is that companies break out by
addressing the fundamentals.

The problem very often is that manufacturers address
symptoms, not causes. We realise, for example, that the market
wants delivery in four weeks when it takes us six weeks to make
the product. We therefore try to guess what the customers will
want, because clearly we have to start manufacturing before we
know what the orders will be. Then we find we're guessing
wrong, so we lay in all sorts of expensive systems to get ourselves
better at forecasting.

But the problem is not bad forecasting, it's the fact that it takes
too long to make things. *That's* the issue that needs to be
addressed, as Toyota realised.

All this is not easy. It takes nerve and the courage of your
convictions. It also needs a rare ability in handling people. If

your production manager is a dyed-in-the-wool proponent of long batches and you've now decided that you no longer value long batches, mind how you break it to him!

Remember, also, that rapid response only works if every part of your operation is geared up for it. Essentially you're adding service to the basic product by giving the customer what he wants very quickly. That service has a number of components, and I think they're worth looking at in turn.

The first is *rapid product development* to allow you to respond swiftly to market need. The key, in many cases, is to switch from doing things serially to doing them in parallel. Conventionally, for example, a product is almost fully developed before the packaging people get a look in. Wouldn't it be faster to give the packaging designers a rough idea of the size early on and get them working simultaneously?

More risky, perhaps, but potentially more profitable if it gets you to market sooner.

The second component is *rapid manufacturing*, which is, basically, making your throughput more efficient. When product flows through factories, you're typically working on it for a relatively short space of time, and the rest of the time it's lying about gathering dust. If you can cut the lying-about time, the whole lot will flow faster. That means smaller batch sizes, which in turn calls for Just-in-Time techniques and faster change-overs. The key there, as we've seen, is having the will to do it.

The third is *rapid information*, and it feeds back into the first two. It helps rapid product development by enabling you to travel from design, to tooling, to manufacture without having to re-key any of the information along the way. And it is of course central to rapid manufacturing, where the effective use of information can take any number of forms.

A company called Linn Products in Scotland has a reputation for producing extremely good hi-fi components. To quality it has now added service by abandoning fixed production lines and creating an infinitely flexible factory. The clever thing here is the use of information technology in the stores area. Having made a few turntables, for example, an assembly worker can press a button marked 'speakers' and a few minutes later an automatic vehicle finds its way to his bench with all the pieces and equipment he needs to get going.

You may not need that degree of sophistication: indeed a cardinal rule is to be no more sophisticated than is absolutely necessary. It may be apocryphal, but I've heard of people buying robots to do painting jobs when all they needed was a fixed jet and a few different-shaped masks for the thing to spray through. Be aware, however, that some very clever techniques are available.

The fourth component is *rapid distribution*. However fast your manufacturing, the benefit is lost if the product tips out into a slow distribution system. Here again, information technology has a big part to play. The courier company, Federal Express, has transformed its business by introducing systems that can tell it minute by minute which of a hundred thousand parcels is on which van in which city.

As we might expect, applying IT to the distribution process feeds back into the way companies make things. Benetton, the Italian knitwear manufacturer, has systems in place that can tell it almost instantly which colours are selling in which outlets. So if mauve is going down well in Milan, it knows to send more. But that's only useful if the factory itself can respond quickly. Benetton cracked that one by the brilliant stroke of reversing the production process. Traditionally, garments were knitted from ready-dyed fibre. Benetton decided to knit them first and dye them as the orders come in.

Simple, but revolutionary. Some refinement has been needed in the dyeing process, but essentially all Benetton has done is refuse, like Toyota, to be bound by traditional thinking.

The last is *rapid management*, which means having an organisational structure that allows you to make quick decisions. You can test how far you've got by asking yourself some questions. Are there people low down in the organisation who are trained and have authority to make decisions? Do you recruit with a desire for change, or to preserve the status quo? Do people get to the top by making improvements or by not making mistakes? Does your structure encourage or inhibit quick decisions?

A business, like an army advancing in the line, can only move at the pace of its slowest unit. There is no point investing heavily in Just-in-Time if it takes forever to develop your products, or having wonderful IT if your distribution is a mess.

The whole approach must be integrated. When it is, the results can be dramatic.

Lastly, break-out is not a once and for all. You may need one rapid advance to get back into the game, but don't then forget to keep moving. The race is to the swift and it never ends.

· 15 ·

Total Quality: How do You Get it?

The story of Japan's industrial renaissance is well known. In the years immediately following World War II, Japanese companies were renowned for cheap and shoddy goods, but in the 1950s a US statistician, Dr W. Edwards Deming, visited Japan to explain his concept of quality and its central importance to economic growth. His audience were top industrialists and they listened to him.

Japanese industry was rebuilt almost from the start with quality in mind. With a few notable exceptions it took US companies another 30 years (and European companies even longer) to appreciate the significance of what the Japanese were doing. The rest of the world looked for explanations of the 'Japanese miracle' in that country's culture, in consensus management – almost anywhere but in the basic attention to quality that had been exported to Japan by Dr Deming.

There is little need to detail the Japanese achievement. Suffice it to say that Japan now controls 50 per cent or more of world trade in over 30 distinct product fields, including semiconductors, shipbuilding, photocopiers, zips, hi-fi, robotics, video recorders, pianos and clocks and watches.

The result has been that whole industries in the West have gone to the wall or been reduced to a fraction of their former size. For most companies in Europe and the USA, achieving quality (or Total Quality as it tends to be termed) is now nothing less than a matter of survival. 'Ignoring the quality issue is tantamount to corporate suicide,' was how John A. Young,

Hewlett-Packard's President, put it. His company is one of a number that have embraced Total Quality principles in recent years, companies that include IBM, Procter & Gamble, Mercedes Benz, Federal Express, Jaguar, British Airways and my own company, PA.

I don't want to dwell on the dangers of ignoring Total Quality, so let's look briefly at some of the benefits it has brought to non-Japanese companies. Hewlett-Packard, for example, found that product failure dropped by 60 per cent and R&D cycle time by 35 per cent, while productivity rose by 90 per cent. Jaguar increased productivity between 1980 and 1986 from 1.3 cars per man to four cars per man. Similarly, Harley Davidson's productivity rose by 50 per cent, and their inventory was dramatically cut by 75 per cent. Caterpillar Tractors claim directly attributable savings of $100 million over the seven years of their quality programme.

These results amply demonstrate, I think, the importance of Total Quality. And it's important not just in an economic sense. In a world of infinite needs and finite resources the elimination of unnecessary waste, which is one of the key features of Total Quality Management (TQM), is a social imperative. But whether or not you adopt TQM, your competition will. How will you manage if they increase productivity by 90 per cent?

Defining Total Quality

In understanding what Total Quality means, it is important to strip the word 'quality' of some of the connotations it has recently acquired. Largely as a result of advertising, quality has come to suggest expense. Designer clothes; the reassuring clunk of the door of an expensive car; made-to-measure brogues; gold jewellery; these are the sort of things that spring to mind when quality is mentioned.

This is misleading. The nut that fits exactly onto its bolt, turning easily but not loosely on the thread, has as much quality as the most expensive, hand-built car. After all, it's components like that nut that go to make up the car. Engineers would describe the nut as 'conforming to specification', but this is not a very useful definition of quality in the wider context of the marketplace. If the customer doesn't want to buy it, it really doesn't matter whether it conforms to specification or not.

What matters, then, is how the customer feels. Quality is judged by reference not to the product or service but to the customer who buys or uses it. So Total Quality is simply defined as 'meeting customer requirements'. Although frequently qualified in various ways, this is the message at the heart of the Total Quality concept.

This definition is broader than it first appears, because the customer is not just the end-user, the person the company sells to. There are plenty of customers within the company. Everyone in the chain of operations is regarded as both customer and supplier, and should be receiving from the previous stage exactly what is needed to do a proper job and handing on precisely what the next person requires. In this way 'meeting customer requirements' gets embedded throughout the company's operations and everyone becomes responsible for getting it right first time. You build in quality as you go along, rather than waiting for the inspection stage to discover whether it's there or not.

The old maxim, 'Do as you would be done by', is a fair summation of the attitude involved here. This means also treating your external suppliers properly, not forcing them to cut prices to a bare minimum just because you've got the muscle to do so, but paying them fairly and promptly and expecting quality goods and services in return; treating them, in fact, the way you want your customers to treat you.

TQM, which is the way you turn your company into a Total Quality organisation, can be quite a revolution. No longer are sales and profits the ultimate goals, with customers seen as those annoying people, always complaining, that you have to pander to in order to achieve them. When 'meeting customer requirements' becomes the central aim of the company, sales and profits should rise as a byproduct.

Adopting Total Quality Management

There are a large number of specialised techniques for introducing Total Quality to a company. This is not the place to go into them in detail, but I would like to touch on some of the general principles.

Many Total Quality gurus begin by saying that management must take command and that the exercise should be driven from the top. This is true. Becoming a Total Quality organisation so often requires such a fundamental change in the way things are done that, to be successful, management, and especially the Chief Executive, must be fully committed to it. But, before we look at the role of management, it's important to look at some of the changes required.

In *The Wealth of Nations*, Adam Smith used the example of a pin factory to show how, by breaking down a skilled job into its many unskilled constituent parts, productivity could be dramatically increased. The division of labour had arrived but, with it, the de-skilling of labour.

Henry Ford, by breaking the manufacturing process down into the smallest number of constituent parts (7,882 in the case of the Model T), deliberately and avowedly exiled not only skill but also humanity from the shop floor. This is a perfect example of the antithesis of a Total Quality company, but unfortunately much of the thinking behind it persists today.

It's such a waste. If you want unthinking machines to do the job, use machines. Human beings have so much more to offer. Nine times out of ten, if you want to know how a job could be done better, ask the person who's doing it. But to get him to volunteer that information, you've got to get him to feel it's worth it, to feel involved with what he's doing. In other words, he has to care.

Volvo did this by moving away from the Henry Ford production-line principle and having small groups of workers building each car. Immediately there was a far greater sense of responsibility. Each worker now knew which cars were his and, if they didn't perform, it was his job to know why.

Once people begin to care about the quality of their work, they not only make sure that their output is up to scratch, they also put pressure on whoever is providing them with input. The individual improvements are often minuscule, but the aggregate of thousands of small improvements can have a dramatic effect on performance. The key thing is that everyone looks for improvements within their own range and is given the means to effect them.

A typical feature of Total Quality organisations is the large number of employee suggestions, most of which are adopted. Japanese examples have been cited elsewhere in this book, but many organisations in the west can point to comparable successes. Over three years at the Fresno office of the Internal Revenue Service in the USA, employee suggestions saved the IRS over $2.75 million.

This is one of the areas in which senior management has to help. They need to ensure that there is a structure which enables and encourages employee suggestions. Indeed this idea of enabling and encouraging is exactly what is required of management. You don't get people to care about their work or be involved with it by ordering or exhorting them. You have to motivate and empower them.

Telling people to make improvements is not enough. Even their desire to do so may not be enough. They must be given the systems and techniques they need to sort out the problems and put them right. Sophisticated methods exist for flow-charting the work processes, understanding the variabilities, planning the functions, and so on. Know what they can do for you and use them where appropriate.

One aspect of TQM that involves you, the CEO, is theme setting. You need to set between one and three themes a year to act as the overall guiding principle for the next few months. These might refer to specific areas where improvement is required, or they might be more general.

Some of my own managers recently attended a presentation from Komatsu on just this topic. A Komatsu representative was asked how they chose the theme to work on. He pointed to a notice board on which was pinned a series of themes – one from the corporation president, one from the manager of the business and one from the plant manager. Each took the same principle but carried it down to a greater level of detail. It was now up to the individual unit to provide its own interpretation.

Somebody then asked: 'What's your target?'

'Three per cent improvement,' was the reply. No surprises there, until one of the interpreters stepped forward.

'I think you've misunderstood,' she said. 'He means, three per cent improvement per month.'

This illustrates an important feature of Total Quality

Management: improvement must be continuous. In one sense, a Total Quality organisation is striving for perfection, a state that is by definition unattainable. There is always room to do something better. Yet it is often the case that companies start down the Total Quality road and, after perhaps two years, either they stop and sit back, thinking, 'Right that's it. We've got Total Quality now. We can relax,' or they reach a point where the return/effort ratio falls off to such an extent that they give up. If that's the position your company's in, don't despair. This next part is for you.

The road to Total Quality

Becoming a Total Quality organisation is not easy, nor is it quick. It's a long, hard road and, inevitably, some fall by the wayside. At PA we've come across a number of companies that have run into difficulties and lost all their original impetus.

From our experience we've analysed four distinct stages on the road to Total Quality, each defined by certain characteristics. I think it's worth briefly looking at these stages here, because the very first thing to do, if you're one of those who's made a start towards Total Quality and then got lost, is to find out where you are.

The first stage we've called Quality Awareness. Here there are a small number of quality champions quietly trying to spread the message. The CEO has accepted that quality is an issue which must be addressed, and high visibility has been given to inspection data. Quality has been defined in terms of customer satisfaction, but only superficially; the customer is still seen as the person the company sells to; as yet there is no recognition of the internal customers. For the moment concrete, quantifiable results are pretty thin on the ground.

In the second stage, Quality Promotion, the overall vision is in place. The CEO, though, is still the prime mover, typically chairing a Steering Committee to oversee the quality programme. The idea of continuous improvement has been introduced, together with specific quality-inspired initiatives such as problem-solving projects, cross-functional teams and education and training programmes. But quality remains what people in the company are trying to *do*, not what the company *is*. There have been benefits, some considerable, but the structures and systems of the company are essentially unchanged.

Stage three, Quality Management, represents a very significant step forward. One, two or three themes are being used to focus the company on areas in which top management want breakthrough results. Quality has become integral to the very nature of the company and no longer an external objective. People talk about 'cutting the re-tooling time on this process down from 60 hours to six' rather than 'meeting customer requirements', not because they've forgotten about it but because it's become so integral to everything they do. Continuous improvement is now an ingrained part of a manager's functions. Quality has become virtually self-sustaining.

The final stage, Quality Empowerment, sees everyone in the company automatically acting along quality lines. There is a very high level of trust and delegation. There is very open, honest communication, both internally, and externally with customers and suppliers. Management is no longer issuing directives from the top down but creating an environment and providing the resources to nurture initiatives coming from the bottom up.

The relevance of these four stages lies in the fact that the road to Total Quality is not a continuous uphill path. This may be true within each stage, but the stages themselves are discrete sections of the road. What this means is that towards the end of a stage the effort required to move further towards Total Quality seems to increase, while the benefits decrease.

This is when so many companies run into problems. As the benefits lessen, so does their morale and with it the drive to go on. They either give up, believing that Total Quality is unattainable or they stop and try to consolidate the gains they've made. The problem is that, if you're not moving forward, you almost inevitably regress. What needs to be realised is that it is at this point, when things seem most difficult, that you should get ready for that surge of effort that will catapult you up to the next stage.

It is during these difficult periods, at the boundaries between stages, that you, as CEO, must take the lead, particularly in the area of morale. You have to believe yourself that further moves towards Total Quality are possible and to transfer that belief to the rest of the company. You must motivate them so that the 'critical mass' of commitment is achieved that will allow the jump up to the next stage.

One of the prime causes of morale loss on the road to Total Quality is an underestimation of the time it will take. To arrive at the fourth stage generally takes at least five years, if not considerably longer. To avoid a loss of morale later, it's vital to recognise that and accept it at the start.

In all of this, it's important to remember why you're doing it. Total Quality is not an end, it's a means towards satisfying your customers in order to achieve a stronger competitive position. For all your efforts, if your customers aren't satisfied, you can't claim Total Quality. So keep your sights on what the customer wants.

A few years back, Procter & Gamble, who had implemented Total Quality very thoroughly, discovered that its Pampers nappies were losing market share to the rival Huggies brand. The company knew its own product was at least as good, so it did some research to discover the problem. What emerged was that customers valued the clear information on the Huggies pack. The requirement, in other words, was broader than product quality – it encompassed service, helpfulness, communication.

So what is the overall role of the Chief Executive in all this? It amounts, really, to a subtle, almost contradictory, blend of standing back and stepping forward.

You cannot implement Total Quality by controlling and commanding, as many companies have tried to do. The traditional pyramid – management at the top, workers along the bottom taking orders – simply will not work. The pyramid has to be inverted. At the top should be the workers, facing out to the customers. Underneath should be the management, whose job it is to support, enable and remove the problems that prevent the workers doing a good job. 'Your servants, the management' is the kind of thinking that must be inculcated.

Yet paradoxically, Total Quality requires the CEO to exercise far greater influence in his company than ever was the case in the past. He needs to achieve nothing less than a fundamental change of culture.

That's not easy. It's what I talk about in Chapter 22.

Making Things Happen

· 16 ·

Strategy is Making Things Happen

Strategy is about deciding where you want to be and ensuring you get there. All strategic thought should be anchored to reality at all times. It begins with facts (where are we now?) and it ends with making things happen. Be as theoretical as you like in between, but don't let go of those two anchors.

After all, most managers do not say, 'How about a new strategy today?' They come to the subject out of real events and with real objectives. 'We've got to grow. . . . If only we could get our act together. . . . Let's re-think what we're doing. . . . If we don't change we're done for . . .' These are the imperatives that typically drive a company's strategic thinking and the exercise is worthless if it doesn't, in the end, address them.

I've known companies spend enormous time and effort working out 'the strategy', then filing it away on a shelf and assuming the job was done. 'We have a strategy,' they say. 'No you don't,' is the rejoinder. 'You have an intention. It isn't a strategy until it has changed something.'

Better to have a strategy which is 50 per cent brilliant and 100 per cent implemented than the other way round.

So let's look at how you keep your strategy anchored so that it actually does you some good.

Analysis

You cannot formulate strategy until you've first analysed the situation you're in. Opinion clearly has a part to play in formulating corporate strategy, but it must rest on a bedrock of fact. Otherwise your strategic decisions are as likely to be influenced by politics or people's preconceptions as by anything more substantial.

The starting point for most companies is a re-examination of their own industry. Who is competing with whom? Who is succeeding? What are the forces for change? How will the industry be different in five years' time?

It may sound obvious, but it's important to identify which industry you're in. If you're making electric drills, for instance, you should not limit your analysis to other drill manufacturers. You're actually in the hole-making industry, and it's conceivable that the next threat could come from lasers or a clever variant of the hammer and nail.

Analysis of the industry needs to be balanced by a careful look at the market. Your competitors may be doing X, Y and Z, but are they meeting the need? Is there an opportunity that nobody else is exploiting? Should *you* be the first with a laser drill?

In answering such questions it is always tempting to play down the opposition and overstate your competitive position. You must always be ruthlessly honest, especially if you suspect you're losing market share.

Formulation

So you've got your facts. The question now is, what are you going to do about them? What will your strategy be in the light of what you've discovered?

Conventional wisdom has it that there are two strategies for competitive advantage. One is make it cheaper; the other is make it different. Broadly that's true, though the low-cost route is less and less an option for companies in the West. Someone in China or the Philippines can usually produce more cheaply. The key, almost always, is differentiation.

There the field is wide open. Indeed much of this book is about how to differentiate your business in one way or another. Your products, your technology, your marketing, your staffing, your systems, everything you've got, in fact, can be brought into play to create a strategy that marks your company out as different.

This is where cleverness and flair come into their own. And

don't overlook the sideways glance, the connection that nobody else has made.

PA once had a client that made matches. Its analysis told the company that its product was losing ground to cheap butane lighters. Question: what can a match company do when people are no longer buying matches? Answer: use the same equipment to make small sticks with seeds on and start selling them to gardeners. That's what it did and it went on to build a successful business.

Strategy formulation is not just about the competitive position you want to achieve; it's about what the business will feel like when you get there, about the people you will have, their values, their capabilities, and how they will work together and sustain the new position.

Implementation

Whatever strategic course you take, make sure you can implement it.

Fidel Castro's first revolution was a failure. Various rebel groups were sitting in the mountains above Havana, and Fidel and his brother Ramon decided they might as well start. They stormed into Havana, Ramon got killed, and the attack was driven off. Meanwhile the others – Che Guevara among them – stood back and watched, refusing to commit themselves until they saw which way the campaign went.

Fidel learned his lesson. Before he tried again, he made sure that all the rebel factions were jointly committed. Then he did it properly.

The moral is, get your people and resources lined up before you start the revolution. If you don't, the enterprise will degenerate into guerrilla warfare.

Where most strategies go wrong is in the implementation. The difficulty is not so much deciding which is the best way to go; the question is whether the company can go that way fast enough. Whichever way you go, it will always be a race, and companies are frequently unrealistic about the time and effort they have to devote to implementing the changes required. The commonest error is to misjudge the difficulty of altering culture and attitudes. All too often, particularly if the planned change is a big one, the results come out half-baked.

This is not a truth to discover by trial and error. By the time you're wiser, you'll be very much greyer. You should think about it hard before you begin. After years of experience PA has become convinced that the critical factor in developing a company's strategy is a realistic assessment of its ability to put it into practice.

Suppose your company is somewhat traditional, and the strategy says it's going to become a dynamic organisation whose unique competence is its marketing thrust. The difficulty of implementing that is colossal, and before you decide to go down that route, you ought to look in detail at all the implications. Does it mean, for instance, that you get rid of all your managers, and if it does, where are you going to find new ones? A strategy can only be implemented by people, and it's awfully easy to make impractical assumptions about the extent to which your staff can redirect their understanding and talents in the new direction. The obstacles that will be thrown up on the human front should never be under-estimated.

What companies too often do is blast away at their strategy on all fronts. They try to do everything immediately and end up doing nothing well. Always take it in *phases*. Accept the realities of the time-scales involved. First, form a detailed picture of the sort of company you will be once the strategy is in position, and then think of all the changes that this will entail – to people, skills, processes, resources – and then work out how you will make those changes occur. And only then begin.

So don't simply pick a strategy out of the air and then decide how you will turn it into action. The process has to be two-way. The what will certainly determine the how, but the how to some extent determines the what. First you must think about the changes required, and once you've decided what's possible, that influences the strategy you pick.

The reason for putting it this way round is that *any* alteration of strategic direction, if it's to be successful, will necessitate a mass of interlocking changes throughout the organisation. And this is the hard bit. To some degree every function will be involved – personnel, production, finance, marketing, research – and every aspect of your activities is bound to be touched in some way: performance, values, organisation, systems, processes. The effort is so widespread that a very great number of things can go wrong with it. Getting things started is a problem. Inevitably, people drag their feet. Middle managers filter instructions to suit their own ends. Some parts of the programme move faster than others, so synchronisation is lost. Unexpected hitches emerge, delays occur, benefits fail to materialise, communication breaks down, targets disappear into mist. Nobody, it seems, has enough time to think through the problems and sort out priorities. Everyone starts to lose heart, and in due course inertia returns, with nothing more achieved than a few partial improvements.

The *management of change*, therefore, becomes the crucial task which the CEO must address, and without it there's no real hope of success. Here I'd like to commend to you three ideas.

In the first place, the management of the change process should not be mixed up with the management of the business itself. Change management is a different task from line management. The two should be kept quite separate and given to different people. The change team, moreover, should report direct to the CEO, who must control and drive the whole project.

Secondly, prior analysis and planning are crucial. All the elements of change required must be identified before you begin, and its implementation must occur in a comprehensive programme which meshes all the moving parts together. This programme must clarify three things. It must define the end in view, the *vision* that your strategy aims to achieve; it must set a plan for the *transition* of the company, by stages, towards that end; and it must specify the means of *execution*, explaining how the various initiatives will be managed and linked together.

The third point I'd choose to emphasise is the very great importance of marking out this journey with milestones. The phases of transition just mentioned above – I call them 'intermediate islands' – can hardly be too well defined. Each of these staging posts should have a particular objective. This should not be a pious slogan but a specific set of improvements, expressed in business terms – increased market share, a structural change, a new process. The objective should be defined both in terms of improved output and the inputs required to make it happen; and of course it should be thoroughly communicated. Everyone in the company should know what has to be done, by when, and by whom. This breaking up of the programme into visible and easily comprehensible steps is essential to progress. Without it any attempt at strategic change is likely to degenerate into a dispiriting, open-ended shambles.

The CEO's role

The management of change has now become a science in its own right: a measure of its growing importance to business. All sorts of techniques have been devised to assist the formulation and implementation of strategy, to ease it and plan it and integrate it through every level of the company. But perhaps these will not be available to you. It's not unusual for a chief executive in a small firm to be facing these tasks on his own. However, with a bit of reflection and common sense, there's no reason why he should not get it right. The principles of good strategic thinking, in large companies or small, come down to a few simple rules of thumb:

- Look carefully at the impact of the strategy on every aspect of the business. Leave nothing out.
- Ask yourself what the practical problems will be. Can they be surmounted – and how? Permit no fudged answers.
- Ask yourself how long the changes will take. Can you move fast enough to match the competition?
- Don't start something you can't finish. Plan each step of the process, and only then begin.

In any case, here as elsewhere, the final decision is yours. However much expert advice is to hand, only you in the end can determine your company's strategy. You will be the judge of its practicality; your vision, your drive are what will make it happen. This is one of those tasks so integral to proper business leadership that you can't pass it to anyone else.

It's true that in some larger companies there will be a Strategic Planning Director, but he will often be a line man. Shell, for instance, doesn't allow anyone to hold this post unless he's been

20 years in the business. To keep its plans rooted in the practical realities, it goes for an experienced manager who happens to have a strategic cast of mind. In many companies, however, the job goes to a professional strategist, in which case it's up to others to bring that realism to the table.

Either way, the onus is on the chief executive to satisfy himself that the strategy is do-able, that the difficulties in it have been accepted, and that everybody understands the inputs required to make it happen.

Outside the confines of the boardroom, your own main priority will be communication. When Jan Carlzon was preparing his overhaul of the airline, SAS, he reckoned that he spent a quarter of his time simply explaining the programme to people in the organisation. The true leader is the one who can communicate a vision.

The second priority is to get your managers involved at every level, and from very early on. There's no point in developing a strategy behind closed doors, then passing it out with a sticker attached saying PLEASE IMPLEMENT. It simply won't get done. Your people must feel they *own* the strategy: only then will they be committed to it.

Ideally, the development of corporate strategy is not a once-off but a constant and incremental process. People tend to think of strategy within a specified time-frame, but it's really about direction. You may need the big turn now and then, but more often it's a case of little tugs on the wheel to keep you heading the right way. The best-run companies are those that constantly analyse and constantly adjust as the world around them changes.

· 17 ·

Mergers and Acquisitions: Are They Taking Us Where We Want to Go?

Mergers and acquisitions have become such a regular feature of modern business life that we refer to them in short. M&A, like P&L or R&D, needs no translation. The abbreviation has entered common parlance.

For the chief executive of a large public company or a small private one, this must now be considered a compulsory item on the agenda. Done right, acquisitions can build competitive strength – in people, in products, in market position. Done wrong, they can ruin your business. As a method of accelerated growth, they have to be carefully considered and fully understood. Few CEOs will get through their stint without at least having to think about a merger or acquisition.

The worst thing you can do, though, is to act from haste, or impulse, or a personal bee in your bonnet. Surprisingly often a corporate marriage is the outcome of a brief, hot, reckless love affair. An acquisition, equally, can be triggered by hostile emotion.

This is never wise. Contested or not, acquisitions should always be the outcome of cool, objective study. As I've mentioned elsewhere, some startling errors of judgement occurred in the run-up to financial deregulation in London. Suddenly it seemed important to most of the banks that they should be able to deal in securities and there was a competitive scramble to purchase jobbing and stockbroking firms. Some of the earlier acquisitions were sound, but later, as the fever mounted, there were hasty and ill-considered decisions; some very high prices were paid, with disastrous results.

Strategic choices

The only defence against such errors is to make quite certain that your own acquisitions sit square with your company's strategy. What will you really, in the end, get out of this merger or that acquisition? Will it take you closer to your chosen business objectives? Or is there perhaps some other, better way?

Such questions should always be rigorously asked, and they have to be answered at three strategic levels:

- *Corporate strategy* governs the acquisitions and divestments of a multi-business corporation. 'Does our portfolio contain the right mixture of businesses? What new businesses should be acquired, which existing ones discarded?'
- *Business strategy* is concerned with the competitive position of each individual business in its market. 'How do we grow this business – organically or through acquisitions? How do we improve its market share? What do we need to invest in it?'
- *Operational strategy* is concerned with inputs made by particular functions – IT, Technology, Human Resources – in support of the business strategy. 'What technology do we need to succeed in this market? Can we develop it ourselves or should we seek it through a merger?'

A sound decision will require an input from all three strategic levels, interacting with each other, top-down and bottom-up. It's your job to see that this occurs, so that any hunches or preferences of your own are thoroughly tested against other views.

On the other hand you shouldn't be too self-effacing. In a crunch, top-down direction must prevail over bottom-up initiative. Acquisitions are so risky and time-consuming, so hard to unscramble when they go wrong, that you can't afford to have your people galloping all over the field at will. As chief executive you ought to exert a strong influence on the sort of deals looked for, and the best way to do it is to set out some general criteria for making acquisitions. These can be expressed in terms of the size of the company, the type of company, the profitability level and cash flow, the quality of management desired and the degree of salvage you're willing to contemplate. It's important to issue some guidelines, however simple, or people will get excited with the pursuit and end up proposing something unsuitable.

Strategy and criteria determine the nature of the search. If you take a decision to grow through acquisition, you must define your candidates carefully, decide where they're likely to be found, then appoint a team to go and look for them. All this should be driven from the top; and that means the chief executive, who should always reserve to himself the final decision, yes or no, on any proposition that emerges.

Search and negotiation

The starting-point for any acquisition must be a clear strategic decision, but at this point it's usually worth pausing to ask yourself, one last time, whether an acquisition is the *only* route to your objective. Might you achieve what you want by collaborating with another company in pursuit of some limited mutual interest? Such alliances are now common practice in the motor industry.

But assuming an acquisition is necessary, the process must now move on a stage. Companies have different ways of addressing acquisitions, but usually a special team is put together composed of financial, planning and technical people, with outside advisers helping if necessary. Their first job is to track through the industry, looking for suitable candidates. Once a target for merger or acquisition has been identified, its financial position and technological base must be thoroughly checked. You have to be sure what you're getting. 'Due diligence', indeed, requires you by law not to throw away your shareholders' money on a dud.

There are two key steps in acquisitions: there's making them, and there's making them work. Different skills apply at each stage. Making them is a curious mixture of procedure and flair. You need to know exactly what you're doing at each stage, and you ought to have a set way of doing it; at the same time there should be an element of creativeness in the way you approach the final deal. When it comes to the point, there are many ways of doing a deal. But you've got to be rigid about the stages and steps you go through beforehand, because if you leave something out, if you haven't checked everything properly, you're heading for certain trouble. So you've got to have the discipline to go through these steps, and it's worth drawing up a strict company rulebook to make sure that all these preliminaries, in which you will not be personally involved, are done right.

Assuming the investigations of your search team reveal no flaw, there will come a moment when you're looking at your chosen target but negotiations have not yet begun. Here's one chance to reconsider. Inevitably, the acquisition won't be a perfect fit. Mixed in with the attractions will be drawbacks, and it's often worth assessing them one last time, measuring the plus factors against the minus.

What will this company bring you that you don't have already and can't get by any other means? What, exactly, are you buying here? Technology? Product? Research base? Market share? A brand? A person? A building? Better distribution? What's the cost, and is it worth it? How much of a premium are you paying for a successful reputation? How much are you buying that you *don't* want and will have to find a way to discard? How much will it cost, in management time as well as money, to integrate this company and raise it to the standard of your own?

If the green light still shines, you have done all you can. Pick up the telephone and make an appointment. But don't get too excited yet. You may be given a dusty answer, or the first meeting may reveal a terminal flaw overlooked by your prior research.

To be repulsed is disappointing, given the hard work and high expectations which always precede a first approach. But perhaps you should be relieved.

You probably know that most acquisitions fail. Around 70 per cent come to grief within a few years, either failing to meet the purchaser's requirements, or ceasing to perform as well as before, or not delivering the synergies expected.

Now why should that be?

I believe there are two common reasons. One is a failure of analysis, the other a lack of communication.

The dangers of poor communication

The communication problem is the simpler. It can happen in the biggest PLCs, but it's more likely to occur in mergers or friendly acquisitions between private companies. The essence of such deals – what distinguishes them from the hostile public bid – is that the principals remain in place. Two sets of owners, two sets of managers, are agreeing to get together and work as one. The smooth collaboration of this newly formed team is obviously critical to success.

Yet the fact is they often fall out. Further down the road, long after the deal is done, the two sides discover they want different things, for themselves or for the company. Each has a hidden agenda which somehow never surfaced in the negotiations. One side wants income, the other wants capital growth . . . One is aiming for public flotation, the other not . . . One wants growth at any price, the other an easy life . . . One sees the company as a downmarket volume producer, the other thinks it should occupy a specialist niche . . .

The differences which come to light can be surprisingly fundamental. Perhaps they were glossed over in negotiations, each side privately hoping that its view would prevail in due course. But just as often, I'm afraid, a conflict of view fails to surface because no one thought – or dared – to ask the simplest, basic questions.

There is really no excuse for this, and it's something that you, as chief executive of one side or the other, can easily put right. Ask the basic questions yourself, out loud and early on. 'Before we get down to detail, I suggest that each of us states, as fully and frankly as he can, what he wants for himself and how he sees the future of the company . . .'

Or something like that. Negotiations, unlike the preliminaries, can't be carried out to a fixed procedure. They call for flexibility and judgement, and they demand your involvement. No two deals are alike; each will be closed in a different way. But if you allow the big questions to be skipped, you will almost certainly be making a bad mistake. However it's done, each side must put all its cards on the table. Unless agreement is reached in total frankness, with every difficulty opened up and talked through, there will be no lasting success.

The private, owner-managed business is perhaps more prone to this sort of mistake than the multi-business PLC. But the latter is by no means immune to failures of communication, and when they occur, the damage is worse.

As chief executive of a public company you must keep your shareholders well informed, and never is this more important than when you're making an acquisition. Your own explanation of the bid's rationale – the immediate benefits to be had, the future potential to be unlocked – will be the main influence on shareholders' decisions, both in your own company and the one being purchased. Some will take their money and run, but others, persuaded by you, will back the acquisition with stock. And to them you must deliver what you say. Institutional investors, especially, will hold you personally responsible for the success of your company's acquisitions. If they feel they've been misinformed or let down, they will promptly withdraw their support, sometimes with terminal consequences.

These hazards and constraints can outweigh the advantages of public quotation. To a fast-moving entrepreneur, they can be an intolerable burden. Richard Branson of Virgin thought so, as did Andrew Lloyd-Webber of the Really Useful Company. Each took his company off the market, exasperated by what seemed to them the limited faith of the City.

Failures of communication can threaten the success of mergers and acquisitions. It's the CEO's task to keep the principal shareholders on board, whether the company is private or public.

The dangers of illusory synergy

But what of the second common cause of failure? I described it as a lapse of analysis. It occurs much earlier in the process; it is more fundamental, harder to spot, and potentially more dangerous. Its name is false synergy.

There *is* such a thing as synergy – it's not just a buzzword – and if you get it right, it can bring real extra value to your shareholders. But you may have to work very hard to realise it. Most acquisitions that come unstuck do so because the synergy which prompted them is only apparent. It does not stand up in practice. This is always a painful discovery, and usually it could have been predicted by some sharper analysis at an early stage.

Vertical integration is a frequent lure. Looking at the value chain in its product, wanting more in its own hands, a distribution company will go into manufacturing. 'We're closer to the customer,' they tell themselves, 'we understand the market, so we can beat the competition.' What they *don't* understand is manufacturing, and how much it differs from retail. So instead of riding on a wave of synergy they find themselves grappling with a business whose drivers are totally foreign to them.

Or, just as easy, you can get it wrong horizontally, as Saatchi & Saatchi did.

Such blunders are all too common. As the CEO of a multi-business corporation, shuffling its portfolio this way and that, false synergies will flit across your vision like bright dancing butterflies. It is this, more than anything, which differentiates your job from that of running a unitary business – and makes it more difficult. Your only defence is a sharp eye for superficial reasoning, an absolute insistence on rigorous analysis.

And there's one good rule you can apply.

Take a closer look at some acquisitions that failed – your own or other people's – and you'll find, I think, that many were based upon a similarity of product, or process, or technology. Such likenesses should never be mistaken for synergy. In acquiring a company you must always look hard at the *market it serves*, and compare it to your own, because that's where true dynamic synergy is to be found.

Time and again, a merger or acquisition will be proposed to the board because of some easy-to-see similarity. 'We understand the product', someone will say. 'We understand the process, the outlets, the sources of supply. We understand the technology . . .'

'Yes, yes,' you must interrupt, 'but do we understand the *market*?'

Make sure that question gets asked. And if there's no answer, beware.

A good example of how to do it right is the company which made copper wire for telecommunications and TV cables. Instead of saying 'We're in the wires business, let's expand that way,' it had the wit to see that it was in the communications business and needed to break into fibre optics. The result was a successful acquisition, based on the realisation that its true interests lay in the market it served.

Business is no more tidy than life, of course. There are no simple, fail-safe, all-purpose rules for mergers and acquisitions. But if you can strip out the hidden agendas and fanciful synergies, you'll have reduced the margin for error.

Integration

There are all sorts of ways to look at two businesses before you put them together. You should study the market fit, the people fit, the culture fit. You should certainly draw up a joint business plan for the future, but the most important step of all is to hammer out between you, *before you even start*, a programme of integration.

Most acquisitions come apart because these basic things are not done properly – particularly the integration. People don't bother to think about the snags of integration. They leave open who's going to run what part of the business, who'll be the boss of whom. They leave open whether two units are going to be rationalised into one, how a customer network will be carved up, how clients are going to be serviced, and it is the horrors of dealing with these things after the event that causes so much disillusion.

It is here, more than anywhere, that the chief executive can make a personal contribution to the success of his company's acquisitions. While the deal is still being discussed, and well before it is closed, you should insist that an integration plan is drawn up. This doesn't mean that you should take part in the detail of negotiation – that may be best left to others – but you should certainly be involved enough in the talking to ensure that the mission and the strategies of the two organisations really are compatible. You must also have a thorough private sort-out with your opposite number, the other CEO. If the two of you don't get on and the chemistry is not right – this has happened to me several times in proposed acquisitions by PA – there is not much point in talking further and the deal is better called off.

What matters is that integration should be thought out. You don't have to do every bit of this yourself; just ensure that it is well planned and well executed. You'll have a part to play, but yours is a steering role; you shouldn't get lost in the detail. Above all you shouldn't have to spend time fire-fighting after the event, which you certainly will do if there are issues left smouldering.

Once the deal is done, integration becomes a change-management task of the sort I described in the previous chapter. If there's one certain thing that can be said about an acquisition, it is that some change will be caused to both parties. And if, as often happens, big improvements are required from the company purchased, the rate at which you can make that change happen is crucial to success. Do it too fast and the deal may fall apart. Do it too slowly and you won't get the benefits; you may have a cosy relationship, but the deal won't bring you the value expected.

All this is chief executive's business. The successful integration of two separate companies, the management of the changes required within each, will make a special call on your powers of leadership. You must demonstrate your commitment to the company acquired; you must make them see your vision for the new merged enterprise, the part they can play in its success, the benefits to them in accepting your authority. They must sign on – and they must stay. The whole new management team must be committed to a common set of corporate objectives.

Without that unity of purpose, your acquisition is likely to fail. And there's a moral aspect too. As CEO you must accept responsibility for all the employees involved in a merger. If you cynically discard the people that you don't require, you will run into trouble and deserve it. Redundancies and divestments deserve as much care as the integration of those remaining.

· 18 ·

Managing High Growth

Perhaps you are the chief executive of a company growing at breakneck speed – in which case this is a chapter for you. Perhaps you are the CEO of a large and sleepy corporation – in which case you might do well to wonder if it's time you stirred things up. More likely, your company is a mixture of these two patterns, and parts of it are growing faster than others – in which case you're probably concerned with balance. How much rope can you allow the fast-growing units, what extra resources can you grant them, without upsetting your other operations?

For all of you, the next few pages should be useful. PA has done some interesting work in this field.

To some extent this is a familiar problem, to which some well-tried solutions exist. Rapid growth requires an entrepreneurial style of management, and large corporations who wish to achieve it have found ways to foster the entrepreneurs in their midst – or intrapreneurs, as a recent book called them, to distinguish them from the more venturesome types who will never accept any corporate umbrella.

Many ways exist to encourage your intrapreneurs. Some of the largest and longest-established companies, such as ICI and Unilever, have devolved decision-making outwards into a number of smaller satellite businesses, each responsible for its own profit and growth. Except for certain budgetary constraints and strategic guidelines imposed from the centre, the businesses are given operational independence. Their managers are expected and encouraged to act like entrepreneurs.

Such methods, together with a drastic strip-down of head offices, were widely adopted by corporations in the 1980s, and they have had a good measure of success. It is simply no longer true to say that a large commercial organisation inevitably stifles initiative. As well as devolved business units, there are many ways of digging out the intrapreneurs and bringing them on. It can be done by participative mechanisms, a flatter hierarchy, protecting those who dare to stick their necks out, and rapid weeding out of dead wood. Such methods will have a strong effect, and they can be reinforced by less tangible inducements built into a company's ethos and cultural norms.

In all this, your own attitude will be crucial. By far the most influential factor in creating a bold, risk-taking, growth-oriented atmosphere will be your own vision as chief executive. Everyone must know that this is the kind of company you want, and they must be often reminded of it. If you can create the right climate, such talent will rise to the surface like trout taking flies. And don't assume it is restricted to management. There may well be some valuable intrapreneurs lying hidden in the depths of your company.

Tohru Moriya is a good example. A middle manager who had recently returned to Tokyo from the London office of JAL, Moriya was permitted to relieve the boredom of a routine job in personnel by revamping JAL's three in-flight magazines, which were losing $345,000 a year. He combined them into one, which is now sold on the streets as well as given away in-flight. It makes a substantial profit and serves as a vehicle for JAL's mail-order service.

Now Moriya has branched out further. After producing *The Stewardess Book*, which became a runaway best-seller in Japan, he set up a cultural centre offering seminars to foreign business-men who were interested in moving to Japan.

All this, mind, was done beneath the corporate umbrella of JAL. In fact the centre has one of the highest profits-per-employee of any operation within the airline.

To find the Moriyas inside your own company, you will need to create an atmosphere in which employees feel free to take risks or propose controversial ideas without fear of being put down. They must be given the freedom to achieve their own goals and job satisfaction.

Your own task will then be to keep the balance. Ground rules must be set which leave room for initiative but retain a measure of control. Resources must be provided – time, money, information – to the movers and shakers, yet not so lavishly that the rest of the organisation is unduly weakened.

The special nature of high growth

So far, so good. All these are things you can and should do to encourage growth within your own company. All are popular techniques with large, well-established corporations who wish to dispel bureaucratic inertia – and they can have an important effect. Corporate arthritis is a state of mind, not a question of size or age.

Nonetheless, there are limits to which the organisation can be bent to accommodate the talented maverick. In the end, you will find, this man and his high-growing unit will either be curbed or break loose. The most you can hope to do is create conditions in which it will thrive as long as possible, then manage the normalisation or divestment effectively.

The reason behind these limits is a simple one. It's the fundamental difference of behaviour required in a fast-growth company. The culture is different, the assumptions, the methods, the values, goals and motivations are all quite different from those that apply in ordinary business. The very nature of the activity is different, in short, and those who succeed in it are a special breed. That is why you won't turn a sleepy company into a dynamic one – or, indeed, put a dynamic one to sleep. You might as well try to turn a tortoise into a hare.

The special nature of high growth has been closely studied by PA in a recent programme of research directed from our office in Malmo, Sweden. The focus was placed on companies in Europe whose sales had grown organically by at least 25 per cent per annum for at least five years. Of the 120 companies examined, some were independent operations and some were divisions of larger companies. None employed less than 200 people.

A great deal of commonality was found among these companies, from which some useful guidance can be drawn. At least 90 per cent of them, for instance, go through a life-cycle of which the dominant feature is crisis. It begins with crisis and ends with crisis, going through intermittent crises along the way. Typically, this cycle will have five phases:

- *The Seeking Phase.* High-growth entrepreneurs will usually try a variety of ideas, one after the other, until they find the unique market concept that permits rapid growth. Many companies fail before this happens.
- *The Impossible Task.* Then comes the big opportunity: too good for the company to miss, yet way beyond its existing capacity. Putting together the resources to deliver is the first crisis met by the entrepreneur and his team. An extra infusion of cash, through loans or investment capital, is often required at this stage – and the impact of success is immense. The company becomes imbued with self-confidence and a readiness to take further risks. A we-can-do-anything mythology is born, which draws in like-minded recruits.
- *Rapid Growth.* From here on, the company's career can best be described as controlled turbulence. New opportunities are quickly exploited. Each brings its own set of minor crises and subsequent short-term plateaux. Decisions are made in a hurry; cash-hunger probably remains an issue. The company grows much faster than its market but sticks to the concept that launched its success.
- *The Final Crisis.* In nine cases out of ten, this erratic progress is halted by a terminal crisis, which can arise for many reasons. The business concept can lose its focus; soaring sales can lead to failures of quality; or, very often, the market simply matures. The opportunities for fast growth dry up.
- *Return to stability.* Until now, the overriding priority has been to get the product out. Other problems have been given a quick, temporary fix. But when growth stops, these problems catch up. While the cash flow slows down, for example, the costs of growth run on. The company becomes obsessed by its difficulties but knows no other way of doing things, so can't find a self-preserving strategy. At this stage investors or the holding company, pressing for a return to profit, will normally appoint a new CEO. To save the company, he has to change its culture, but in doing so he destroys the elements that fuelled its extraordinary growth. Key people quit or are

fired. Within a few years the original management team has gone, along with half the staff. The company settles back into the stable condition of a typical, well-ordered, slow-growing organisation.

This, then, is the roller-coaster ride imposed by really high growth. There are, it seems, few exceptions to it. But despite its inherent instability, high growth can be successfully managed. It has its own rules, and they need to be understood. In this kind of business, just like any other, there are winning strategies to be had.

Strategies for high growth

The process should begin with a deliberate, strategic decision to acquire a dominant share of a growing niche market as soon as possible. The need to do it quickly comes from the simple fact that market share costs least in the early stages of the game. Once the market has matured, share will only be increased by heavy expenditure on branding or new technology or acquisitions.

Having found a niche to grow in, the company must then work hard to make that growth happen, putting resources into capacity before the market fully develops. This takes courage, and can often lead to problems of cash flow. But the investment forces the company's sales and marketing people to achieve the necessary volume.

This ability to think volume at an early stage, which marks all successful high-growth companies, has a secondary but important effect. It obliges the company to focus on its core business. There simply isn't time to do anything else.

Coping with continuous demand for more volume is the recurring crisis of high-growth companies, and it forces them into all sorts of expedients. They have to find quick ways of widening their distribution and expanding their capacity. This will often lead them into hurried acquisitions, alliances and joint ventures, a strategy in which there are always two dangers: loss of control and loss of quality.

Finally, cash flow: the lifeblood of expansion. Skill in controlling it is another key to success. But while they need good financial management, high-growth companies are not good at coping with pressure from owners or shareholders to generate increasing profits year on year. In their own eyes, this isn't what they're about. Growth is what they're about, if necessary at the expense of short-term profit. If part of a larger company, they will often try to shield their performance from scrutiny, distrusting the short-term vision of the corporate bean-counters. This of course upsets the bean-counters, which is often the first step to terminal crisis.

Rules for the CEO

Suppose, now, that yours is a high-growth company. What guidelines are there for a chief executive? Not many: that's the quick answer. But a few. This game, by its nature, has less rules than most, but PA's research has gone some way towards defining the critical faculties of a high-achieving, entrepreneurial CEO.

At the heart of them is his ability to master conditions of hectic change. He has to achieve the kind of balance between anarchy and bureaucracy that will maximise growth at an acceptable risk. Too far one way, and the company loses momentum; too far the other, and it slips beyond control.

You will need unusual strength of vision to hold the company on track. You will have to delegate as many decisions as you can while keeping tight control of those you can't. To solve each crisis as it occurs, you will have to be flexible, shifting the focus of priority from one short-term target to another. You will need to foster informal systems of control, setting guidelines rather than hard-and-fast rules. Your gift is to create an organisation which is more of a network than a hierarchy. You avoid job descriptions, because they're too static; instead, you find the people to fill the job spaces.

The whole of the company's structure is shaped around people rather than functions – and that's the way you like it. You encourage the formation of project teams, who develop the mentality of bomber crews as they hit one impossible target after another. Knowing that in your sort of company a shortage of resources is a sign of health, you become expert at making do. You only hire new people when the need is really urgent. You keep administration to a bare minimum.

Around yourself – and this is vital – you form a management bomber crew. You need a united, loyal team who share your own vision, but it must contain a careful balance of skills, including someone who knows when to stop. In every fast-growing company there has to be a hard-headed realist.

Rules for the parent company

Suppose, now, that you're the CEO of a large corporation of which this fast-growing unit is simply a division or subsidiary. Straight away the game alters. Other, more subtle skills are required of you, and some delicate judgements.

In the first place, you, even more than those directly employed in it, need a thorough understanding of the high-growth process: how it works, what drives it, the ways it can go wrong. Because you know how different this unit is from the rest of your business, you don't apply the same criteria to it. You may indeed have set it up from the start as a separate cell, so that it could flourish in its own special fashion.

You're prepared for its fluctuating profit performance, because you know that the path of high growth is never smooth. You have explained this to your executive colleagues and divisional managers. From a high-growth unit, you have argued, any profit contribution is a bonus: the real payback comes from the growth in asset value.

In this and other ways, you may need to protect the fast-growing baby from its parent corporation.

But one day there'll come a point when it is the parent that needs protecting. Once its growth falters, the high-growth unit can no longer expect any preferential treatment. Your problem is then what to do with it. To merge it with another, more mature operation is almost always a mistake. The clash of cultures is too great.

At this point you must be prepared to accept the sale of the business or a buy-out. Another solution is to reshape the business as a mature unit with more formal controls, but in that case you shouldn't expect the original team to stay with it. The smart thing is to have another mission impossible ready, to which your bomber crew can transfer.

Some people were born for the stress and strain of high growth. The instant decisions, the freedom of action, the terrible hours – it is all meat and drink to them.

Their enthusiasm, naturally, can lead them into folly. They can ruin your company or do great things for it. The trick is to point them in the right direction.

Taking Care of Your Image

· 19 ·

Image and Reality

Like it or not, your company presents an image to the outside world. All who have ever been in contact with your business – as shareholders, as staff, as customers, as people walking past in the street – will have formed some sort of perception of the kind of company you are. And it's not just your logo and letterheads that proclaim your identity. More often it's the little things like how well the car park is signposted or the way the staff answer the telephone.

So the trick is not to *create* an image, because your company's image already exists. The important thing is to control it.

The trouble is, image-making is such an amorphous activity it's hard to know where to begin. Would your **PR** budget be better spent giving parties for deprived children or putting your logo on a hot-air balloon? How much should you be spending anyway? And who's to say whether *anything* you do will make any difference?

Thankfully, more can be measured than most people think, and a little structured thinking can go a long way to defining what actually needs to be done.

The first step is to define your audience. For your business to get from where you are to where you intend to take it, who are the people you most need to impress? The answer may not be obvious. True, no company can get very far unless it enjoys good standing with its customers and shareholders, but what about the local residents, or the partners of your staff, or the planning authorities, or potential recruits, any of whom might have an influence over how well your business does?

Your corporate strategy will determine your target audiences. Decide who they are and don't limit your thinking to one or two obvious categories.

Once you've chosen your audiences, don't second-guess them. You may think you know what your image is, but you could be wrong. In my experience there is no substitute for going out and asking people what they think of you.

You need to know what people *actually* think of you, and you need to decide how you *want* them to think of you. Easy enough, you might think. But again it can pay to do some research.

At one stage in its history, PA asked clients and potential clients what most influenced their choice of consultant. We got a string of answers back – having the best people, having technical expertise, giving value for money and so on – and as a result we were able to prioritise the messages we had to put across. For example, clients placed a high value on getting the right consultant, as opposed to breadth of services offered, so we knew that our breadth would only be valued if we used it to assign the most appropriate consultant to each specific project.

At the same time we asked our clients how they actually saw us. Some of the answers were not what we expected – or wanted! For example, many of our respondents did not see the relationship between various parts of PA. We're actually the largest European-owned consultancy, but people were seeing us as a series of niche practices. This discrepancy at least showed us what our communications task was.

Essentially, then, PR is about closing the gap between the way people think of you now and the way you'd like them to think of you in the future. And in setting your target image, do give it some strategic thought. The message you project can be very finely tuned – and indeed should be, or you're missing an opportunity. It can mark you out as progressive, traditional, homely, high-tech, one of the herd, one *against* the herd, and so on. Do you, for example, wish to be identified with, or disassociated from, your parent or subsidiaries? Notice how all P&O companies are stamped with the same distinctive logo, while Rupert Murdoch's newspapers appear to do everything possible to *avoid* being identified with one another.

It's strategy that dictates; and for that reason you, the chief executive, must be involved in defining the target image. To help you decide, you may like to bring in gurus from the PR world, but the message you finally choose must be yours.

Once you know what people think of you, and how your company wants to be perceived there is a third aspect to be borne in mind – obvious, but sometimes overlooked – and that is the reality of the situation. Don't depict your company as high-tech if you know it isn't and never will be. You'll lose credibility faster than you know. The same goes for any other sort of attribute, however desirable it may be.

To my mind, that's where British Rail went wrong with its short-lived slogan 'We're getting there'. It contradicted people's existing perception of BR; as an aspiration, it was too apologetic to inspire much confidence; and it didn't match reality, since most people felt there was little improvement.

With all this under your belt, you can start prioritising your activities. Give your PR people an infinite budget and they'll still ask for ten per cent more, but if the choice is between parties for children or your logo on a balloon, you at least have some questions you can ask. Does it address the right audience? Does it help close the gap between your desired and existing image? Is it true to the kind of company you *really* are? If none of those, then don't do it. Think of something else.

As to how much you should spend, there is no rule to be had. It depends on the type of business you're in and the size of the task undertaken. However you will certainly have to spend in a crisis. Great or small, crises hit every company now and then, and PR, properly handled, can be a powerful weapon.

Perrier spent a fortune recalling every bottle of its famous water because of a benzine scare. The company had no choice; its success depends on the concept of a totally pure product, so if the purity is questioned it *has* to be seen to be taking action. Time will tell whether this much-publicised recall and relaunch can win the company more business than was lost by the original scare. It sometimes happens: witness the Tylenol case in Chapter 8. However it turns out, Perrier's fast and public action is undoubtedly better PR than Exxon's long silence after one of its oil tankers polluted the coast of Alaska.

I don't propose to dwell on crisis PR. It's a skill in itself and there are very good specialists who can help you. All I would say is, if a crisis strikes, get yourself the best advice you can. A crisis PR specialist will stop you following your first panic impulse and will help you devise a cool, rational response. Better still, take action *before* the crisis; go through the 'what ifs?' and plan your response in advance.

Crisis or otherwise, you need to keep track of progress. Having done your base research, carry out more research at intervals to see how well you're doing. If nothing else, it'll tell you when it's safe – or not safe – to ease up on the spending.

In PR there are no short cuts. It's tempting to look for the gimmick, the philosopher's stone, that will suddenly cast your company in a favourable glow. It doesn't exist. There is nothing for it but hard graft to raise your image notch by notch, and I reckon it takes three years from a standing start to achieve any noticeable difference.

But you can have a lot of fun along the way. Structured and disciplined programmes, far from quenching creativity, often help to release it.

Two questions to conclude with.

One: how much should you yourself be doing to make yourself famous? It's important here to distinguish strategy from execution. You can't escape responsibility for strategy – and, to some extent, for execution, if it's you the media want to interview. So improve your competence through coaching and a good scriptwriter. Further than that, perform if you're good at it and don't if not. (I know at least one captain of industry whose PR people do all they can to keep him away from the media.) If it's not your forte, find colleagues who are good at communicating and bring them forward.

Two: do you need an outside PR agency? My advice is go outside for technical expertise and a certain amount of strategic thinking, particularly in a crisis. Much of the rest can be done in-house, with the advantage that your own people are full-time for you and not marking things up. In either case, you, the chief executive, must manage your company's PR and provide its central message. Your executive team can only amplify your signal. If there is no signal, the amplifier just sits and hums. So make sure there is one.

· 20 ·

Investor Relations: To Be Loved, You Must Communicate

I must start this chapter with a disclaimer. I have no personal experience of running a public company. As this book goes to press, PA Consulting Group is not quoted on the Stock Exchange. Although a flotation is planned, a firm date has not been decided, and so I still enjoy the relatively sheltered position of CEO in a private company.

However, the demands made by investors and shareholders on the CEO of a publicly quoted company is not a matter this book can ignore. It is one of the most important challenges he faces and it makes a big claim on his time.

And there are some useful things to be said.

My qualification for saying them rests on the experience acquired by PA of advising public companies. Secondly, I have the benefit of our own survey – the one I mentioned at the start – in which we asked a sample of chief executives to give us their views on financial relations. It was a subject on which they had plenty to say and practically spoke with one voice. So let's start with their views, and then see what's left to add.

The facts of life

The respondents were agreed that the dramatic increase in shares held by private individuals in the UK is a good thing, correctly encouraged by the government during the 1980s. However, it has made little difference to the average PLC. Many of the newcomers to the stock market only hold a few shares in one or two companies, whereas the overall proportion of listed shares held by financial institutions has actually risen, and now stands at over 80 per cent.

This is the dominant fact of life for the chief executives we questioned. As one of them said, 'The institutional investors are the owners of the business, when all is said and done.'

'I am very concerned with institutional investors and the analysts and brokers who advise them,' said another, whose comments summed up the consensus. 'I devote a high proportion of my time to communicating with them, seeing them, talking to them and ensuring that they are informed about what we are and what we are doing. If they understand what we're about, they react in an appropriate manner.'

This was the general view. All were agreed that this line of communication could no longer be left to sporadic or casual contacts, but had to be part of a planned and continuous programme. 'In exactly the same way that one has to take a much more targeted approach to customers,' added one respondent, 'one has also to take a more targeted approach with investors.'

Notice the tone of acceptance in these remarks, the lack of complaint. None of the CEOs questioned felt that regular briefings for investors were an unfair call on his time. As one of them said, 'You can't get the support you want from shareholders unless you talk to them.' Another felt the process had not gone far enough. Chief executives in the UK, he thought, spent less time on investor relations than their counterparts in the USA. 'This is something we need to step up.'

Are these men typical of CEOs at large? I certainly hope so. I agree with every word they say. The stock market is an integral feature of any developed free economy, and along with the pressures and constraints it imposes, come great advantages and opportunities. Complaining about it is useless. The challenge is to understand it and use it to your company's advantage.

Short term versus long

So what of the charge, quite often heard in the US and the UK, that the financial markets impose their short-term view upon industry to the detriment of long-term industrial planning?

Short-termism, as they call it, has been trotted out as an explanation for all sorts of economic ills. I remain sceptical. Though not without a grain of truth, it is a misleading simplification. It serves more often as an excuse for failure than a solid explanation of events.

Of course the financial markets can't ignore the short term. Shares are traded by the day, the hour, the minute. But it is worth noting that much of this activity is among the market-makers. The institutions themselves are not big position-takers. Their portfolios don't alter dramatically from day to day but are subject to small adjustments, as you'd expect from prudent management. And quite right too. The institutions' prime loyalty is to the people whose money they hold. If you had a pension with an institution, the last thing you'd want to hear is that it had been gambled for a quick gain. Nor, for that matter, would you rejoice to know that it had been parked with a company for whom the institution felt a sentimental attachment.

The truth is the City itself is continually balancing the short term against the long. And its analysts are not stupid people. They have good memories and they keep bulky files. They remember what you said at your AGM three years ago and they wonder why you still haven't done it. They notice, also, when you *do* turn your plans into action, and they bear that in mind when you tell them what you plan to do next. When it comes to making judgements about the longer term, they look for integrity and consistency, a coherent strategy, a good track record. And the ones who follow your company closely will know a lot about it. In some respects they may even know more than you do, because their perspective is broader, very often international, and they're always assessing you against the competition in your market.

Are these people to be regarded as a blight on the nation's industrial development? To me the charge seems both silly and unfair. More to the point, it was roundly dismissed by the chief executives interviewed in our survey. Only a minority mentioned a conflict between the long and short view, although they agreed that the institutions were a demanding bunch. 'The market is unforgiving,' said one. 'It looks for jam today as well as jam tomorrow.'

However, the prevailing opinion was clear. The onus rested

on industry to explain itself, rather than on the City to change its ways. As one of our respondents said, 'If your business is understood and they realise what you are planning for the long term, you will find the institutions are more patient and accommodating than conventional wisdom has it.'

Another was even stronger on the point. 'If shareholders are properly informed, there need be no conflict between short and long-term views.'

In any case, said several others, the market is right to demand jam today as well as jam tomorrow. In a well-run company, however good the plans, satisfactory annual results still have to be achieved. 'No major conflict in seen between short-term profits and long-term planning,' said the main proponent of the view. 'I believe entirely in having a strategy for the company, but you have got to know, year in, year out, that you are hitting your targets. Otherwise you go broke.'

The chief executive's role

To digress from our own survey for a moment, one of the most illuminating documents that exists on this subject is a survey carried out for the London *Evening Standard* by Dewe Rogerson in 1986. Its research, which was designed to shed light on the efficiency of corporate communications, included interviews with industrial leaders, stockbrokers, fund managers, directors of merchant banks, financial journalists, MPs and shareholding members of the public. The sample was substantial – in all, nearly 600 people were questioned – and no-one has ever disputed the authority of the results. One of the questions asked was: 'What are the major factors you take into account when making an overall assessment of a company?'

Of 11 factors mentioned in reply, one came out clearly top. Quality of management, said 64 per cent of the sample, was the most important factor. The even more interesting thing is how strongly this view was held in the City. Of the stockbrokers, merchant bankers and fund managers questioned, *over 90 per cent* said that quality of management was the most important factor in their assessment of a company.

The 30 chief executives in our own survey agreed that what the City rates highest is quality of management. Asked what particular qualities were valued, they mentioned four. Confidence came first, they thought, then a good grip of what is going on; the CEO's personal involvement in strategic thinking was important, and so was his commitment to the strategy that resulted. There must be no suspicion, in other words, that he has lost a battle in a boardroom or will wander off to another PLC at the first twitch of a headhunter's eyebrows.

The upshot of all this is clear. It is you, the CEO, who must take charge of investor and shareholder relations. Only you can do it, because it is you who make the difference. It is you the company will be judged by, whether you like it or not.

This responsibility can often be shared with the Chairman, if you've got one, and the Finance Director. The balance of roles and personalities at the top will vary from company to company.

But this doesn't alter the fact that you are the key figure. Shareholders, investors, bankers, brokers and reporters all expect the CEO to lead his company. They won't be satisfied with anyone else.

Ways and means

When it comes to investor relations, you can't be a shrinking violet. One way or another you have to project yourself, and, through yourself, your company. Good communication is essential, but there's room for variations of method and style. You should choose those that suit you best.

Regular, small, informal meetings with your major institutional shareholders are a must. Other investors should be seen from time to time, and you should make yourself available on request to the leading analysts.

How you handle these encounters will depend on your personal style. Not everyone can manage the up-front approach of big personalities like Alan Sugar or Robert Maxwell. There are plenty of successful companies where the management is more collective, and consciously presented so.

Dewe Rogerson's survey revealed a connection between familiarity and popularity. The better known a company is, the more highly it will tend to be regarded. This assertion seems undeniable, if unremarkable. Much less deserving of credence, however, is the idea going around that a high-profile, headline-grabbing CEO is good for his company's share price. The career of John Harvey-Jones at ICI is cited as evidence, but that is not enough to support the theory.

PA's own adviser on investor relations does not set much store by it, anyway. A high public profile is fine, he says, so long as things are going well. In bad times it does not help. What it does do, probably, is increase the volatility of your share price.

This sounds like good sense to me.

Another interesting comment he makes is that in an investor relations campaign, just like any other, you need to define your objectives. Do you want your stock highly valued or not? Do you want to be seen as a go-go, fast-growing company or one of rock-like stability? In marketing terms it is known as positioning. It applies to this field too.

Whatever positioning you select, it can't be allowed to vary with every breeze that blows. Your relations with investors and shareholders should be part of a consistent strategy of corporate communications. You will only achieve credibility and impact by repeating the same message over and over, in bad times as well as good.

The temptation is to relax the communications effort when things are going well, but the penalty can be severe. It is no good suddenly appealing for support when things go wrong and you're faced with a hostile bid. By then it will be too late. Your support should be grounded on a clear understanding of your company's strategies, already put into position by years of patient exposition.

What the papers say

Your general exposure in the press is bound to have an important effect on your standing in the financial community. People may have a precise mental image of your company but may not be able to say where they got it. The chances are they got it from the press.

So you can't afford to bark 'No comment' every time you glimpse a shorthand pad or a microphone. You don't have to manufacture things to say, but if there is something to explain and you can, you should. If you refuse to tell journalists anything, they will make something up, and it's usually bad.

When people are left in ignorance they always assume the worst, and in an arena like the Stock Exchange, which thrives on daily rumour, a prolonged silence can be disastrous. Unless you do something to pick it up, you will watch your share price drift gently, inexorably down. This is known in the PR business as 'no-news blues'.

So you should try to say something, if possible short and friendly and simple. Always simple. A golden rule, this. Never complicate or convolute. Make up your mind what it is you want to tell them, and say it straightforwardly. What you say should be sensible. It should also, if possible, be interesting. If you want to be quoted, you have to say something a little bit memorable. Put yourself in the reporter's shoes, think of the readers he serves. Try not to say something so bland that nobody could conceivably write it down or be bothered to read it.

There are, however, situations in which silence is enforced on you, either by the law of the land or by the rules of the Stock Exchange. And there are some questions to which the reply should invariably be 'No comment'. For instance, if you ever say 'Yes' or 'No' to questions about acquisitions or disposals, a refusal to say 'Yes' will automatically be taken as 'No', and vice versa. 'I never make comments about acquisitions' is the compulsory response.

This is Lord Hanson's technique, and it's said that he only permits himself one variation of it. When asked if a company is for sale, he will sometimes reply, 'Oh yes, everything's always for sale. How much would you like to pay for it?'

Getting the Best Out of People

· 21 ·

The Company Atmosphere

Every company has its own atmosphere. There are happy companies and there are unhappy companies. The difference can be felt straight away.

This is a chief executive's business.

A company's atmosphere is set, and can only be changed, from the top. If it's bad, the fault is yours, and quick corrective action must be taken. If it's good, bravo. But be sure to keep it so, won't you? Companies are like gardens in this respect. Neglect them, even for a day or two, and up spring the weeds of discontent. If you want to see rows of happy plants, you have to keep tending the soil.

'All happy families are alike,' goes Tolstoy's famous opening line, 'but every unhappy family is unhappy in its own way.' The same is true of companies. Unhappy ones can suffer from too much direction or too little, too much talk or too little, too much structure or too little. Each is a different nightmare.

Happy companies, on the other hand, are alike in two ways. They have good internal communications and a clear lead from the top. Those two features are always present, even if their form varies; and they are indispensable. Take away either and trouble begins.

Lack of internal communication gives rise to rumour and gossip, which is usually the first step towards a miserable atmosphere. People have to talk about something, and if they don't know what's going on, the talk can only turn to tittle-tattle.

Gossip is a part of corporate life, and no-one is ever going to stop it; you might as well try to ban laughter in working hours, as Henry Ford once did. But that doesn't mean you can ignore it entirely. Because gossip can get out of hand. The trouble starts when it becomes malicious or the source of unsettling rumours. If the subject is a person's departure from the company or an organisational change, misinformation can cause real trouble. In the absence of verified fact, people tend to assume things are worse than they are. Alarm and despondency can spread like a bushfire, ignited by a stray remark in the corridor.

To this the only answer is a good system of communication through which the company itself, as opposed to individuals, disseminates information. That way there is at least a supply of fact against which the rumours have to compete.

Since becoming chief executive I have learned that it is almost impossible to over-communicate internally. You can inform people ten times over about the strategic direction of the company, but there will always be someone who claims he wasn't told. Never mind. Say it 11 times. The fact that a few people always fail to get the message is no excuse for not having the best possible internal telegraph.

Vickers is an outstanding company in this regard. Its chief executive, David Plastow, is a passionate believer in good communication. The more information you provide, he argues, the less there is to gossip about. So briefing meetings are held at least once a month throughout the organisation. Strategies forged in the boardroom are not explained just to middle management, but to all employees on the shop floor, who are given time out of the working day to attend the briefings and encouraged to ask questions. Obviously that has a motivating effect. But it also has a levelling effect, which is just as important. When everyone knows what is going on, it isn't easy to say to the next man, 'I know something that you don't know'. The pullers of rank are kept in place.

Good internal communication, in other words, is more than the spread of information. It means creating an atmosphere in which people at every level of the company feel able to express themselves freely without fear of being put down.

The way things are run will always be criticised, especially in organisations staffed by intelligent and creative individuals. The trick is to ensure, first, that criticism is well informed. Second, it should always be constructive, rather than negative and self-serving. Suggestions that are sincerely intended to help the company should always be welcome, whoever they come from and however blunt.

An open style of doing things is now more widespread in business. The mushroom theory of management (keep them in the dark and feed them ****) is slipping out of style, and good riddance. If you want a happy company, let the light in. And if you want to hear good ideas – they come from all quarters – give your people the facts and let them speak up. Otherwise you'll only hear the yes-men and office politicians, who are expert at getting up close and saying what you want to hear.

Office politics! Now there is a sign that a company really has gone wrong. Worse than gossip, worse than rumour, this is a weed to be pulled up by the roots as soon as you spot it in the garden. Especially at board level or just below, politics are a dangerous and destructive menace. There is nothing good to be said for them at all.

So how do you keep this blight in check?

Good internal communication will immediately reduce the danger, because politicians thrive on hierarchical secrecy. In an open atmosphere they have a harder time. Their wiles are more apparent. Self-interest is easily spotted in a roomful of people whose habit is to argue freely and sincerely, even fiercely, about the company's interests. Anyone can see the difference between an honest confrontation and a stab in the back. Another important counter-measure is to make your own feelings clear. The whole company should be aware that the chief executive does not want to hear snide remarks and has a sharp ear for the self-serving opinion. He is so averse to office politicians, in fact, that he takes some trouble to see they don't succeed.

That should be your reputation. And of course your example is even more important. If you yourself engage in office politics, or exploit them for your own ends, you can't expect others to behave any better. Your methods will be imitated, first in the board and then beyond, until the whole company becomes a seething mess of intrigue.

Some executives, like some cabinet ministers, are fond of the inspired leak. But this is a dangerous ruse which easily backfires on the user. Don't do it. In a company which is ably led there is no need for such subterfuge.

Leadership, remember, is the second ingredient in all happy companies. There is no point in having a good communications system if there is nothing to communicate. There has to be a clear lead from the top, because the absence of it creates an atmosphere of uncertainty, a vacuum, which can only fill with mischief. Office politics thrive on uncertainty. If people feel that nothing is decided, therefore everything is up for grabs, they will start to jockey for position, curry favour, form backstairs alliances.

Companies are especially prone to such outbreaks when a change is imminent or badly required. This is always a dangerous period, to be shortened if you can. Grasp the nettle, push the change through, get it settled and announced, so everyone knows where they are again. Once the company has a clear strategic direction, you can ask people to back it or get out. The conspirators have lost their advantage.

Some people, I should add, are politicians in the better sense of the word. They achieve their results indirectly, using influence and discussion rather than tackling their objective head-on. This can be a valuable gift, especially in companies with a flattish structure of command, and it's unfair to call those who have it intriguers. Provided their motive is the company's interest, not their own, and provided their methods don't cause resentment, they should be allowed to do it their way.

Good leadership comes in different styles, and you will have your own. There are not many rules to be had here. Take that old one about MBWA. Management By Walking About, Lord Sieff said, is the mark of a good chief executive, worth more than an MBA. The CEO should get out of his office, see for himself, talk to the people who don't report directly to him.

Like most such rules, it's a bit too simple. I'm a great believer in visiting other people's offices when I want to discuss something, but mere walking about has its dangers. Especially in a hierarchical company, it can be seen by other executives as going behind their backs. So always tell the manager concerned you're visiting his patch and have him come with you if he can.

Certainly, however you do it, you should keep your ear to the ground, because companies have, and always will have, their informal networks of communication, supplementary to the official one. Somewhere in your organisation will be the equivalent of the parish pump, and you'd be well advised to locate it, perhaps even stroll that way from time to time. When I started at Whitbread early in my career, it was said that the gateman knew more than anyone else in the company. On another occasion, when I was visiting Rolls Royce, the driver of the car which met me at the station expressed some surprise at my presence. 'I didn't think you'd be coming today', he said. 'They're busy getting ready to announce some redundancies'. Sure enough, when I reached the main office, the management were tense. 'We will be announcing three hundred redundancies', they explained. 'But this is confidential.'

And that's a good story to end on. Suppose the passenger in that car had been an employee, not a passing consultant. In an unhappy company, he'd have been annoyed or frightened by the driver's state of knowledge. In a happy company, he'd just have laughed.

· 22 ·

Changing Your Company's Culture

In your time as chief executive you will no doubt be instituting all manner of changes in your organisation. Much of the purpose of this book is to help you do just that.

However, the ultimate test of a chief executive's ability probably comes when the culture itself needs changing.

Unless it is unusually dynamic, culture always lags behind change. The company's history, environment, past and present leaders, the type of people it has tended to attract, the size of the organisation, its technology – not to mention the rituals and legends accrued over the years – create a company personality that might, on the one hand, be a very useful resource, but which can also become a drag on the direction you wish to take.

The culture issue is usually thrown into relief when a company faces some sort of shake-up.

Take a merger or acquisition. Where the union is friendly, it is likely that the two companies will have got to know each other over time and to some extent will have absorbed each other's cultures. All the same, as in any marriage, the adjustment can be painful. The German-Dutch aircraft consortium, Fokker-VFW, actually broke up because of cultural incompatibility and a complete misunderstanding of national motivations. When problems arose, the German managers wanted firm guidelines while the Dutch preferred to make up solutions as they went along.

In hostile situations the shock is potentially even greater. Typically, the staff in the company taken over will not want to change their way of doing things to accommodate the new owner. The latter, meanwhile, must either find some way to overcome that reluctance or adapt his own culture to that of the company acquired. Either way, somebody will have to adjust.

On the other hand, the impetus for a cultural change can be purely internal. You're about to embark on some form of break-out and you need your people to think in new ways. Or you've taken the decision to become a Total Quality company and you intend that every part of the organisation should be committed to a new set of values.

Whichever direction you're coming from, only you, the chief executive, can effect the change. And the first requirement is vision.

Vision means just what it says – seeing the company as you intend it to be at some point in the future. What you then must do is get the vision understood by others to the extent that it starts to influence their values and behaviour.

It can't be done in a casual or improvised way. You need a strategy that defines where you are, where you ought to be, and how you will bridge the gap.

One manager who changed his company's culture with notable success is Colin Marshall of British Airways. His own account conveys very clearly a sense of strategy.

'When I joined British Airways, I set a corporate objective to be the best airline in the world. This objective was set against a background of state ownership, morale-sapping losses, over-manning, product-led marketing and poor service.

'It was obvious that our goal to be the best airline would only be achieved over a period of time and could not be an overnight transformation.

'There was a need for a new attitude towards our customers; then for a new style of management; then a change of image.'

In BA's case, the vision was encapsulated in a phrase, 'Putting People First'. That was absolutely the right thing to do. As the saying goes, you can get people to march on a sentence but not on a paragraph. Time and again, I've seen management sitting down to express their mission. As more hands get to work on it, the statement gets longer and longer, with more and more qualifications and concessions, until it reads like the small print on an insurance policy.

'There's our mission. Now march!' says management proudly.

'Can't understand it,' say the staff, if they bother to respond at all.

Moral: give your people a rallying cry, not an exposition.

The next mistake that many companies make is to produce a slogan and stop there. Slapping up exhortations on your vans and company notice boards is useless unless management is taking action to turn them into reality. That again is where British Airways did so well. Colin Marshall restructured his management, changed his corporate identity and produced a memorable advertising campaign. He also involved his staff at every level. In his own words:

'Putting People First' is not a mere marketing slogan. It represents a state of mind required by all the staff in British Airways.

We set out to achieve the support of our staff by inviting them to take part in a series of two-day seminars which showed not only the contribution they could make as individuals, but what they could do in their relationships with customers and colleagues. By the end of summer 1985, all our staff had attended a 'Putting People First' seminar.

The impetus throughout must come from the top. You and your executives must tramp the patch, not just to explain the message (any competent manager can do that) but to show that you believe it and intend to achieve it. As Woody Allen said, '90 per cent of success is turning up.' The fact that somebody important comes in person and explains is very powerful.

The chief executive has to keep agitating, as it were, to keep the ripples spreading through the pond. If he stops, they stop; inertia returns.

Colin Marshall did it by asking of any new proposal 'How will it improve the service to the customer?' Department heads soon realised, without the need for memos or directives, that no proposal would get past the boss unless it addressed this issue. They in turn filtered the message to their own staffs with the injunction, 'Whatever you do, make sure you include proposals on customer service.'

So, because the man at the top constantly asked one relevant question, the message soon began to register that customer service should be at the forefront of everybody's thinking.

Consistency is essential. Every decision you make, every customer contact, every promotion, every investment, must be compatible with the change of culture you're trying to bring about. The doubters – and there'll be many – will be on the look-out for the smallest inconsistency, even a slip in your body language. If you say 'customer first' but tacitly condone a decision which damages a customer, you're done for. The news will spread like wildfire. As chief executive, you must live and breathe the culture change. If you're not committed, no-one else will be, and you shouldn't even start.

· 23 ·

Building a Winning Team

How do you choose the team that will help you run this company of yours?

The place to start is with yourself. Early in your tenure of office – or even before you take office – ask yourself the question, 'What are the critical skills or qualities needed to run this organisation?' Consultancy jargon would call them critical and enabling competences – the enabling being those needed to do the job at all; the critical being the ones that will help you to make a conspicuous success of it. Only you should decide what those competences are, and they'll obviously be different from one company to the next. I would suggest, however, that if you can't answer the question, you should never have taken the job.

Once you have your list, match yourself against it. Which of those skills can you tick off against yourself, and which can you not? Again I'd be surprised if you didn't already have a pretty clear idea of the answers. Few people get to be chief executive without knowing what they're good at.

The problem lies in the gaps – those areas which your own capabilities do not cover.

In some cases, there may be no-one who can fill them but you. If your company needs a high-profile leader giving lots of speeches and constantly going on television, then, like it or not, you as chief executive must take that role. If you're no good at it, you may just have to learn. Richard Branson, when he first started appearing on television, was dreadful, in my view, as I hope he won't mind me saying. But not any more. He recognised that he had to improve and did so.

In other cases, the gaps *can* be filled by your colleagues and the appointments you make ought to complement your own weaker areas. Many chief executives don't find it easy to admit where they're weak, but it must be done if the resulting team is to be an effective one. Don't try doing *anything* – be it running the human resources policy or choosing the pictures for the lobby – if one of your colleagues can do it better and if the job does not need to be done by the chief executive.

So you've identified the particular capabilities you need around you. How then do you fit the people to the jobs?

Obviously you need people who can do the jobs. That goes without saying, and at the top end of the company the talent should be pretty obvious.

But you also need people you can trust. I'm not talking here about whether they're honest, but whether they deliver what they're supposed to deliver on time and without having to be chivvied. Your life as chief executive will be busy enough without having to worry whether jobs are getting done.

There was a gunnery commander in the Eighth Army whose responsibility was to organise a barrage in front of the advancing troops at El Alamein. He discussed it only once with Montgomery, who told him the pattern of shellfire he wanted in the forthcoming battle. During the next six weeks Montgomery never mentioned it again. But the orders hadn't changed. Having said what he wanted done, Montgomery assumed it would happen and moved on to the next thing. Trusting people saves a great deal of time and worry – as long as you have chosen trustworthy people in the first place.

Make sure, as well, that the members of your team are capable of thinking as a team. The brilliant individual who shoots off at tangents can do more harm than good. Be sensitive to any jealousies or dissent that such a person may be stirring up within the group.

All the same, don't limit your team to the stolid and predictable. An effective team comprises both visionaries and plodders – the one to smash preconceptions and open up the lines of sight; the other to curb excesses and provide a realistic counterbalance.

You'll choose your people, obviously, by knowing them. For

my own part, I've also found psychometric evaluation to be a useful check on what I thought I knew. You may feel that it hasn't told you anything you didn't know already, but it has the benefit of being completely objective. It may also alert you to strengths or weaknesses that are worth investigating further before you make a particular appointment.

A key question is whether you should build your team from those already in the organisation or recruit from outside. Personally I favour drawing on internal talent wherever possible. However, a small number of external appointments can be stimulating; and as CEO you have a special responsibility for their success. Without your support, these outside recruits can easily be rejected by the body corporate. They are certain to make mistakes, after all, and so you have to make sure they are not placed in too exposed a position at the start.

Teams are tricky things. You cannot live without them – otherwise you'd be doing everything yourself – but once they exist, they can take on a life of their own and head off in all sorts of directions that may or may not be helpful. Once the team is in place, therefore, your own task is both to motivate and control it.

There is no better motivation than your own example. The old military principle of never asking your subordinates to do anything you wouldn't do yourself is a sound one in business too. After all, they must trust you, just as you must trust them. They must see by your own actions that you are committed to the values and strategies you're putting before them.

Sometimes the need to forge and motivate a team may call for unusual methods. The senior managers of Apple Computers UK all climbed Kilimanjaro. Carnaud of France, having just merged with Metal Box, sent the new management team on an expedition in the Jordanian desert. Most of them had never met; among them were eight nationalities; but after a week living rough together they had formed the necessary bond. The exercise ended at a hotel in Amman, where a mission statement for the new company was drafted.

Possibly your own team lacks some enabling competence. It might be a sense of cohesion; or mutual trust; or familiarity with each others' strengths and weaknesses – or something else altogether. Be imaginative about how you might supply that enabling competence. If cohesion is essential to the success of the business, and a trip up the Amazon is the way to get it, perhaps you should think about it hard.

More conventional, and certainly sufficient for most companies, is to take your team away from the office for a few days so that their environment is changed and they have time to think and discuss the company's future. A lot of companies do it with very helpful results.

You also motivate by stretching your people. The team that developed the Sony D-50 portable disc player was given a block of wood the area of a compact disc jacket and an inch and a half thick – roughly a twentieth the size of Sony's original CD player. That, the team was told, was to be the size of the new player. The initial reaction was that this was impossible. The fact that they succeeded had as much to do with the shattering of preconceptions as with having the technology to do it.

The Sony case was also an exercise in team control. Targets and constraints were very clearly set, and, with those understood, the team was free to do what it liked. Teams get unproductive and restless when they don't know where they're supposed to be going. Set the direction, lead by example, stretch and challenge, and you'll not only keep your people on course, you'll also get the best from the team you've created.

· 24 ·

The Chairman and Non-Executive Directors: A Help or a Hindrance?

As implied by his title, it's the chief executive's job to build his company's executive team. Nobody would argue with that. Not half so clear, however, are his own position and responsibilities *vis-à-vis* his chairman and non-executive directors. This is an area where company practice varies greatly and there are few rules to be had. From the CEO's viewpoint it contains the potential for great help or hindrance, so it's worth getting right.

Perhaps you are, simultaneously, the chairman and chief executive of your company. The positions are often combined, and some notably successful leaders in business hold them both. This arrangement accommodates the big-ego type who hates to share power (how effective he can be!) and it has the great virtue of simplicity: there is no ambiguity about the chain of command. At the time of writing I myself hold both positions in PA. Perhaps it's ego, but I hope not. It can be effective, but it can also lead to role overload, and I would value the comfort of sharing the leadership task with the right chairman.

At the start of this book I said that no chief executive could ask for sympathy in the job, but to that there is one exception. After a really bad day you can take your frustrations to the chairman, who will contribute to their resolution and send you home feeling better. This is no small thing. It gives you more strength for the job.

Even more important, you can seek his advice about a difficult decision. He can tell you what he thinks or you can use him as a sounding-board to help you sort out your mind. Nobody can fill this role better than a chairman. He knows as much about the company as you do, he sees it from nearly (not quite) the same viewpoint as you do. Your relationship with him is close and confidential. There is no other like it.

There are many examples in business, some very well known, of successful two-man teams at the top. When closely inspected, however, I suspect they have no more discernible pattern than friendships. Each is a delicate balance of two personalities, each one a different mix of responsibilities and complementary skills. The partnership has usually developed over years and has its own inimitable chemistry.

Marriage, perhaps, is a better comparison than friendship. Certainly when things go wrong between chairman and chief executive, they can't simply split and go their own way. They are locked together in a web of corporate responsibilities. They can, and often will, continue for years, coexisting miserably until one or other retires or drops dead. I suspect this state of affairs is more common than surface appearances suggest. As with other people's marriages, you never know and can't ask. The first you know something is wrong is when the tension erupts in a messy divorce. This, too, can happen in business.

The moral is clear. The chairman and chief executive are a partnership, and they must be chosen by the board with just the same care as families might take in an arranged marriage. If possible they should already know each other, and preferably they should have worked together over a number of years. It's pointless and disruptive to choose a chairman who will control the chief executive, or vice versa. There must be strong grounds for believing that their personalities will mesh well enough to form a natural, easy team.

Assuming you are part of such a team, the two of you must then agree a division of roles. Such contracts are rarely formal or written down. Often they're not even spoken. They usually develop in a tacit and pragmatic fashion over a period of 18 months to two years.

Another thing needs to be said about the chairman. He can be your friend and confidant, yes, but he's also the man who will fire you if you fail. For this he would probably need the backing of the non-executive directors, but the initiative would come from the chairman, so you're all right if he's on your side.

If he's not, your whole position could be in danger.

This possibility, however remote, always colours the relationship. Even when it's going well, there is a potential for tension within it on which your future could rest. A good chairman will handle this aspect of his role with tact. Even so, it can be a difficult thing for both parties.

All the more reason for having a chairman you know well. A chairman who'll never disagree with you, however, is not worth having at all.

Often, of course, it's the chairman who chooses *you*, the company's chief executive; and sometimes you will be succeeding him in the post. In that case it's doubly important to clarify who does what. Is the chairman executive, non-executive, or something between? Does he intend to run the show with yourself as managing director? Or will you be running the show with help as required from the chairman?

'I'm executive only in the last resort,' he will probably tell you. But what does he mean by that?

Don't accept the job until you get an answer. If no clear answer is forthcoming, there are a number of tests by which the balance of power can be judged. If the incumbent chairman has just dismissed your predecessor without a murmur from the board, then either the fellow was a scoundrel or you will be similarly vulnerable. Another good test is the line responsibility of the Finance Director. If he reports direct to the chairman, then the chairman is in charge, and you will be no more than director of operations.

A third test is strategy. If the chairman keeps charge of it, he is in control. There is no way that you can call yourself a chief executive, or act like one, unless you're in command of corporate strategy.

These are the signs you can easily recognise. There are other clues, hidden, more subtle, by which you can gauge the reality of power, which will never be the same from company to company.

To some extent you'll have to take your chairman on trust and mould your relationship with him as you go along. But before you sign on, it's important to get these matters as straight as you can. Ask the questions; insist on answers; strike a compact on who does what. You need to know what you're getting into, especially with a chairman who claims any sort of executive role.

In my own view, based on the many variations I have seen, the best bet is a non-executive chairman who spends two or three days a week in the job with some clearly defined responsibilities. Internal communications are something he can well oversee; shareholder and media communications are another. The important word in his title, however, is non-executive. He should not be running the company. That is the job of the chief executive, who keeps it unless or until he makes such a hash of it that the life of the company is threatened.

The most successful cases I can think of are those where the chief executive himself has graduated into the post of chairman, temporarily absorbing both jobs perhaps, but eventually handing on the task of CEO to a carefully groomed successor. The people concerned have come to know each other well before a change occurs in their relationship. This evolutionary approach has a much better chance of success, I think, than an outside appointment in either position. We have seen it, with small variations, at Vickers, Thorn EMI and Tate & Lyle.

The division of roles is very much eased, I should add, if each party has clear personal strengths. Many public companies – GEC and Lonrho, for example – have a former politician in the post of chairman with responsibility for relations with the government and City, while executive responsibility rests with a CEO whose skill and experience are beyond challenge.

Another situation which will clarify the roles, perforce and overnight, is a crisis. The company has got into trouble; the chairman and CEO (one of them probably brought in to help) must collaborate to rescue the situation, dividing the most urgent tasks between them. The chairman calms the City while the CEO attacks the operational problems. If they succeed, they'll become a strong team, each fully respecting the role of the other.

Coming now to the non-executive directors, they too can be of great help to a CEO, but only if carefully chosen. Some chairmen will claim the right to appoint them, but this should never be done without your consent: a point you must insist on. As CEO you must take a close, active interest in these appointments, because they can profoundly affect the balance and effectiveness of your board. It's a task that must be worked on.

Nor is it an easy one. You can't choose a non-executive director in the same way as you'd choose a manager; nor does it follow that someone with a good record in management will succeed as a non-executive. The roles are fundamentally different.

Once again we are into an area of great variety, where no established best practice exists. Companies have different traditions; national custom varies too. But there are a few generalisations which I believe are valid.

Firstly, I think you have to be clear about the skills and attributes that you want your non-executives to have. A company becoming more international, for instance, may well seek to broaden the nationalities represented on its board. A company going public may want a director with experience of serving in a PLC. A company with delicate government relations or an environmental problem may seek a non-executive with the relevant experience. As I mentioned earlier, a company reliant on technology may well want a non-executive expert against whom to test the arguments of its own technologists.

And so on. Each non-executive ought to be able to contribute some angle of vision that the board would otherwise lack. This is the only good reason for their presence. I'm not a believer in simply collecting public figures for the glamour they can add to the company's letterhead.

In terms of numbers, unless you are following the US board model, I'd say three is about right. One man alone can't stand up to the board and two are self-cancelling if they disagree. Above three there is the danger of a pressure group. The total should certainly be a minority, relative to the other directors. A board composed entirely of non-executives is too easily control-led by the chairman and CEO, whose advice they must passively accept, not knowing enough about the business to argue. One sees evidence of this in many US companies.

Passive attendance at meetings, punctuated by occasional statements of opinion, is not, in my view, contribution enough. Non-executives ought to take some part in the business, otherwise they start to bore the rest of the board by not understanding the company's jargon or any detailed talk about its activities. Sub-committees of the board, assigned to some particular project, are a good way to initiate them.

Finally, their appointment to the board should always have a term. Non-executives have a natural tendency to self-perpetuation, but you'll need to make changes as the company moves on and develops a need for other outside views.

Non-executive directors, like the chairman, can broaden your vision and strengthen your hand. But they need to be chosen with care. Get it wrong, and you'll be looking with envy at the thrusting young entrepreneur who is answerable to nobody but himself.

· 25 ·

Role and Reward: Don't Be Trapped by Structure

Don't get bogged down in organisational charts. They're useful, of course, in showing who is answerable to whom, but they can very easily take over and undermine what you're trying to achieve.

One problem is that charts divide people who should be talking to each other. In hospitals in America, general physicians and specialist consultants work together on easy terms, while in Britain the latter are treated almost as supermen. The same awkwardness can exist in industry. In many companies 'design' never talks to 'production', and the minds of the two never engage. The chart puts them in different boxes and that's the way they behave.

Charts, secondly, are a breeding ground for office politics. They foster a hierarchical mentality and that latent human desire to knock people off their perches – all of which can be a serious distraction from the business in hand.

The point is, organisational charts should be shaped by the company's market objectives, not vice versa. If the result looks untidy, never mind. What matters is that the job gets done. And as the objectives change, so will the organisation. The chart is always provisional: you never reach a point where it's safe to set it in stone.

The same increasingly applies to pay structures.

Beware the administrator who likes to have rigid rules about who is paid what at which level in the organisation. Usually it's a defence mechanism: it helps him to feel he's in control and managers to feel they can blame the system when their own decisions are questioned.

But that can create all sorts of nonsenses. I've seen companies where individuals need cars to do their jobs but aren't allowed to have them because they're not senior enough; or where the company needs to hire some sort of specialist but can't pay him the market rate because that's what they give to divisional directors.

Like the organisational chart, your remuneration structure should reflect and support whatever it is you want to *achieve*. And it can be made to do so.

You presumably want to maximise your sales: you may well find, however, that while some of your salesmen are going flat out, others are opting for comfort and making do with little more than basic pay. That's possibly not what you intended, in which case you may have to alter the mix of basic and bonus pay. Perhaps if you set the basic a little lower and the bonus higher, the salesforce as a whole will be better motivated and performance will improve. In other words, pay structures *can* be made to support the company's objectives.

At the same time, be aware of what people want. Individuals have different needs. Some are in it for the cash, others prefer part of the package to be in benefits – a car, a development programme, health insurance, whatever. Your administrator may complain that trying to accommodate people's preferences is just too difficult and that it's far simpler to award benefits on the basis of rank. I suspect he's wrong. Nowadays, in fact, there is a growing trend towards the mix of pay and benefits being chosen by the employees themselves. You may need to spend a little more on administrative help, but that's all.

In the 1990s, I believe, this trend towards choice and flexibility will be taken further. In today's labour market the demand for sophisticated skills is such that people are asking more of their employer, expecting more say in their terms and conditions. Any company that wishes to recruit and retain the best people can't afford to ignore these expectations.

So don't be fussy about neatness in your organisation or pay structures. What matters is whether they work.

· 26 ·

Is the Business Suffering from Demotivated Managers?

'I'm old enough that a move would be very difficult. I'm obsolete. I'm at a dead end. There's no way up, no way down and no way out.'
US middle manager, *Business Week* survey, 1988.

'An unmotivated guy in a key position can cost you millions of dollars.'
Daniel P. Weadlock, former President of ITT, Europe.

Yes, it happens. There are times when every manager wants to throw it all in and go fishing. Motivation vanishes. There are no hills left to climb, or, even if there are, there seems little point attempting them because the way ahead is bound to be blocked.

To a point it's inevitable, particularly if you believe C. Northcote Parkinson's dictum that 'in a hierarchy, every employee tends to rise to his own level of incompetence'. In other words, you keep rising until you hit your ceiling, but you can't tell whether you're there until finally you're in a job which you can't do. The result can be thousands of employees all inadequate for the jobs they're in, which is not only depressing for the individuals but bad news for the company.

There is also the awkward fact that pyramids get thinner towards the top. Inevitably there will be some who want to rise further and cannot.

That said, there's a lot you can do to ameliorate the effects of demotivation. Here are three courses of action you may like to consider.

Promote sensibly

The most damaging cases of Parkinson's law tend to occur where promotion goes to the next in line. Those who get the jobs are not the people who can do them best but those who have been around for longest. That's fatal. If it's happening in your organisation, stamp it out at once.

That's rare, however, and getting rarer. Most promotions in most companies do involve a degree of assessment. The trouble is, the process, more often than not, is purely backward-looking. You look at a person's record, at how well he's done in his last three jobs, and you leap from there to assuming he can do the next one. This is not always the case, as many a salesman has found when all of a sudden he becomes a manager of salesmen because he's good at selling. That's a total non-sequitur. He *may* make a good manager, but you can't assume it from his record.

There is a particular risk in taking practitioners out of front-line positions and asking them to do management jobs. The best of ward sisters is not always a good nursing manager; a gifted teacher will often make a poor head of department; the good salesman will often be a terrible sales manager.

Such errors are painful for the people concerned, as well as costly for the organisation. The answer is to do all you can to make assessment more scientific. Look at the job to be filled in terms of its critical and enabling competences. As we saw in Chapter 23, the enabling competences are those the candidate must have to be able to do the job at all, while the critical competences will help him do it exceptionally well. Then compare the requirements with what you know about the candidate, looking not so much at what he has *done* as what he *is*. The difference is important. Instead of building projections on previous performance, you're trying to get down to the basic fibre of the individual. Psychometric evaluation will help. It will also show you which skills might need to be developed once the candidate is in the job to enable him to do it even better.

Promoting sensibly won't in itself stop people getting bored with their jobs, but it will remove that corrosive feeling of self-doubt that many people carry with them.

Tell people where they're going

Managers can react positively or negatively to the fact that they've reached a plateau. Those who cope with it best are people who feel they've had clear, positive feedback; who know they've done a good job for the company; who recognise their limitations; and who have learned early on to take control of their own careers. Those who react badly tend to be managers for whom promotion is very much a matter of status; who have not received adequate assessment and feedback; and who feel that their lack of progress is the company's fault, not theirs.

You can limit the damage by helping people early on to know how they're doing and what they can expect. Even if you can't offer them anything higher, at least allow them to sparkle in the jobs they're in. If you don't already have regular appraisal, think hard about putting it in place. And once you are appraising, make sure you communicate the results. The most embittered individuals are those who have suddenly hit a dead end without being told it was coming. 'If I'd known sooner, I could have done something about it!' is the common cry of a marooned middle manager.

Year-to-year appraisal should be supplemented with career reviews – which are not the same thing. Career reviews take a longer view, looking typically at five to ten years of the individual's career. They're valuable at the pivotal points, namely about three years after the employee achieves his first managerial position and has had the chance to test his capabilities; at around 45 to 50, when there's still time to make a move, and after 50, when the individual is probably on the final straight. (That's less true now than it was, incidentally: demographic change and the shortage of younger skilled people has started to create new opportunities for those at the other end of their careers.)

Career reviews serve a useful double function. As far as possible, they should help people to keep climbing by alerting them to the opportunities best suited to their skills. But they should also give long-range warning of a possible plateau to allow people to prepare in whatever way is appropriate.

As well as telling people where they as individuals are heading, keep them informed about what's happening in the company at large.

On top of that, where companies are cutting back, changing location or bringing in fresh faces, there is always a threat to job security. At middle management level, steps which seem sensible in the boardroom may take on a threatening aspect.

It's common during any restructuring exercise for morale to take a tumble. Minimise the damage by giving ample advance notice of what is going to happen; by making it possible for people to air their views; by offering counselling for those who are going to lose their jobs, and by explaining clearly to those who are staying where the company is going next.

Think role, not rank

Much of what I've suggested so far is a palliative rather than a cure for the problem of managers running out of steam.

The big question is, can you fix it so that people do not become demotivated in the first place?

I think you can.

Management burn-out is most commonly caused by structures based on rank. For bright people, the symptoms typically start to occur in the 40s where the sides of the pyramid are closing in and all that apparently lies ahead is 15 to 20 years of the same thing. They're bored, but they daren't step sideways for fresh experience, because that would be construed as demotion.

What they really need is a change of role – a new canvas to paint on. But the demands of rank forbid it, so they stay put and gradually lose heart.

The key, in my view, is to think less about rank and more about role. What *role* should this or that person be filling in order to enjoy himself and make his best possible contribution to the company's success? If you can put him in it, you'll keep him longer and in 20 years' time he'll probably still be contributing. But you can't do it if your organisation is rank-bound. You must somehow lose the ladder mentality.

You might start by adopting different titles, calling people by what they do rather than where they stand in the hierarchy. If nothing else, this allows you to be much more flexible in whom you hire and how much you pay them.

A role culture allows you to deploy your people to best effect.

It enables experts to flourish. It offers lateral movement to a demotivated person who has been in his job too long but is clinging to his place on the ladder.

Don't, however, underestimate the tenacity of the ladder mentality. If you're serious about removing it, going for roles instead of rank, you may well be looking at nothing less than a change of company culture. Read Chapter 22 before you start!

· 27 ·

Euromanagers:
A New Breed?

As the countries of the European Community combine to form a single market, with monetary and political union coming up behind, it is often the cultural differences that are most noticeable. And long may the differences remain: Europe would be a dull place without them.

However, we shouldn't let differences of language and national temperament obscure the fact that the countries of Europe have a great deal in common. There *is* such a thing as a European culture, and we in Britain share it. For me nothing brings this out more sharply than a visit to the United States, where the culture is deeply different. Language notwithstanding, I would say that Britain has more in common with France than with Texas.

Europe, fundamentally, is an entity. What we're entering, therefore, is an enlarged *domestic* market of the sort that the Americans have enjoyed all along.

And it's important that we use our domestic market as they have done. Much of the talk in Britain is still about going 'into' Europe as though it were foreign territory. That's true to the extent that we're competing for European business with companies based in other countries, but the really important change is the advantage that unity will bring to Europe as a whole, the British included, when it comes to competition with the rest of the world.

Large domestic markets are very useful. Strong local demand for Japanese cars, for example, creates economies of scale that allow Nissan and others to transport quality vehicles half way round the world and still offer them at competitive prices in the UK. Fierce domestic competition and high expectations on the part of domestic consumers have also played a part in ensuring that Japanese companies, when they *do* break out of the home market, are equal to the best in the world. In other words, Japanese companies have used the home market to set themselves up to become world competitors. There is no reason why European companies should not use the new single market in the same way.

Becoming global is now the name of the game in most manufacturing sectors. World-class companies need world markets to generate the revenue to create new generations of world-class products – and the route to world markets is through large domestic markets.

This being so, it is worrying that true Europeans, of the sort we need to exploit the new conditions, are still comparatively rare.

The kind of person I have in mind is a cultural chameleon. I think of a one-time colleague who was brought up in London's docklands long before they became fashionable, and who pitched himself into another world by winning a scholarship to Cambridge where he graduated with a first in classics. He worked for PA when much of our work centred on industrial relations and commuted quite naturally from shop floor to boardroom and back again. I envied him that facility.

The new European should be able to cross national boundaries with the same sort of ease. For that to happen, individuals are needed who can work in several languages and understand the cast of mind from country to country. But there's more to it than that. Companies should be working to produce a pan-European culture of their own – one in which this new breed can flourish.

In PA we've tried to do just that by treating Europe as a single market before it officially becomes one. Other than meeting local fiscal requirements, we record neither profits nor revenues by country. They are simply European. In any case, we'd be hard pressed to allocate them by country. Is a job German because the client is German? Or French because the team leader is French? Or Danish or British because we happen to be using Danish or British specialists? The fact that our own accounting does not attempt to distinguish helps, I believe, to foster a European attitude of mind.

British companies have started to put more effort into this. The high street banks, for example, are investing heavily to encourage the learning of languages. For some time ICI has had a policy of deliberately moving its high fliers from country to country, so that by the time they get to the top they have learned to operate easily across national boundaries.

But these are modest steps by a handful of companies. We can expect this cultural challenge to remain long after the removal of regulatory boundaries, and it ought to be tackled, I feel, with more vigour.

It is in all our interests to produce a new generation who are trained to think of Europe as their territory. They deserve to be noticed, developed and pushed to the top.

· 28 ·

The Art of Smooth Succession

There are, I think, very few companies that have thought through the problem of succession. Most chief executives are not nearly as concerned about long-term development for their first-line executives as they should be.

There is no question that this is part of the chief executive's job. In PA's survey, every chief executive we contacted said he saw it as his responsibility to identify and bring on his successor. Opinions differed, however, on how it should be done.

One view is that it's up to the board to make the appointment, the chief executive's responsibility being to make sure there are good candidates available. One chief executive maintained that it would be wrong for him to train someone specifically because 'it would tend to create a copy of myself.'

The majority view, however, was that the chief executive *should* make a positive recommendation to the board to ensure that it picks 'the most appropriate candidate'. At the John Lewis Partnership, the outgoing chief executive nominates his successor and apparently the board is bound to accept him.

Another executive saw succession as a horse race. 'You must line up those whom you see as possible successors. You then have time to observe them. But you have to reduce the runners to just one or two at least two years before you plan to retire. You need the two years to give him the help he will need.'

Japanese companies have a clear way of handling this. There will be several candidates to succeed the President, or CEO, of a company. One will be chosen and the others will leave to run smaller firms or move into government service. ICI adopts a similar approach. Before a chief executive is appointed, two or three clear candidates have emerged. One gets the job, while the other two move to other companies.

This is all, however, concerned with the final stages. More important than how you select on the day itself is creating a big enough pool of talent in the first place. To achieve that, the work needs to start a long way down the organisation, and a long time in advance of any possible change-over.

It begins, as so much does, with the chief executive sharing his vision of where the company is going and the kind of organisation he sees it being in five, ten or 15 years' time. That vision should influence the kind of people who are recruited – the kind of people who will, indeed, be running the company after you have gone.

Once you're getting good people in (and you've got to get that right first), great care should be taken to develop them. I can't overstate how important this is. What *is* your company if it isn't people?

One of the most successful companies of the last few decades has been IBM. It's not coincidental that IBM also takes its human resources extremely seriously. Even now, in the early 1990s, the company is training 'Team 2000', the executives who will lead IBM into the twenty-first century. A three-tier planning system helps to identify the ten to 15 people who could run a site, function, plant division, country or group in the future. The tiers focus on those who could be in these positions one year, five years and ten years ahead.

IBM, of course, has a huge pool of talent to call upon. Out of a payroll of 387,000 around the world, some 1,600 employees are currently involved in top management and executive training. Even in smaller companies, though, it is important to start to nurture future talent.

With the future a constantly moving target, you need to stay alert to new and different skills that ought to be brought on. For 70 years, the management of a building society has run along traditional lines. Now, with deregulation, there is suddenly a premium on innovation and customer service. The societies that are doing best are those who saw the change coming and made sure the right skills were being developed or recruited.

Nowadays many multinationals have adopted Unilever's policy of deliberately moving its high fliers across national and functional boundaries so that when they become senior managers they will do so with the right experience behind them.

But where does this leave you – today, next week, next month? I'd suggest a few points that are often overlooked but which should be kept in mind:

- Have a good human resources director. Amazingly, many companies still don't see the need for one. Many prefer to tuck the function under 'Finance and Administration', which displays their attitude for all to see.
- Charge your human resources director with knowing the high-fliers – which means both knowing who they are, and knowing them. He can do it better than you, because if the chief executive starts paying too obvious attention to particular individuals, the line managers over them can feel threatened.
- Beware of promoting just the people who catch your eye. From your elevated position, it's easy to notice individuals who happen to pop up over the parapet and create a halo effect around them. It might be a particularly good sale, or a superb performance at a conference or meeting, and the credit may be well deserved. Be careful, however, not to beatify such people at the expense of other good workers who happen to be outside your line of vision.
- Ensure that recruitment to senior positions is not handled exclusively by the candidate's peers. The old adage that people don't recruit people better than themselves is as true as it ever was. Nor are peers qualified to sell the vision of the company you're trying to create.

In the end the mechanics of picking a successor are not that important. What matters is that, over a period of years, a pool of talent has been built up and given the necessary experience and development to run the company in the future.

Whoever follows you, however he was chosen, your last service to the company should be to make it a smooth transition.

· 29 ·

Leadership is All

This book began with markets and ended with people, but it could just as well have been the other way around. The successful company has to get both things right. It must continually adjust itself to every shift in its market, seeking the optimum for its customers; it must also seek the optimum for its employees, continually adjusting its structure and procedures to recruit and retain the best people. Both endeavours are equally important. Success in each depends on success in the other. To be the best in your market, you need the best people.

But good people are scarce and getting scarcer. What's more, they know it. They understand their own value very well, and this confidence is making them more mobile, more choosy, more demanding of their employer. Money alone will not hold them in place. They want job satisfaction, career development, a pleasant environment and the pride of knowing they belong to an elite.

In the last few chapters we have looked at ways these expectations can be met. But in the end it comes down to you – the chief executive. Nothing will be more important in attracting good people to your company, and keeping them, than your own personal example.

What we're talking about is the art of leadership. It has cropped up once or twice in this book, but now we are looking at it clearly as the one thing no company can be without: the single, most important ingredient of corporate success. A good CEO must be a good leader.

In our survey of chief executives, there was widespread agreement that leadership, not management, was the main requirement for the job. Lots of people can manage, and even those who are bad at it can be taught to do it better. Leaders, however, are much rarer and leadership is not easily taught. It's an elusive quality. It has no formula, though we all recognise it when we see it.

Pick any dozen successful leaders in business and you will be instantly struck by the difference in their styles and methods. Some are rampaging autocrats, whereas some achieve results through participation and discussion, the quiet exercise of their own example and influence. I myself have always favoured the second method, but it has its dangers. You can not lead by consensus, I'm quite sure of that and you can't let discussion run too long. In the end the decision is yours and you have to make it stick.

How you do it is up to you. All the same, there are some pointers as to what *constitutes* a leader, and they may help you to decide whether you yourself can claim to be one. Perhaps even here – where there are no quantitive measures to be had, and precious few of any sort – you can raise your performance by thinking hard about what is required.

A leader wills the end, as opposed to a manager, whose talent has more to do with the means. A real leader makes other people want the same end as he does, not by compulsion, but by example or persuasion or some other means more mysterious.

'Leadership', said one of the respondents to our survey, 'is the ability to make up your mind; to stick to the decisions you have made; not to be worried about unpopularity; to be consistent; to be able to communicate and to have a very good knowledge of the business.'

One might refine the comment and say that all successful leaders share three qualities. They have a vision, they have the ability to communicate that vision, and they have the gift of empowering other people to turn the vision into reality.

Most of the decisions you make as a chief executive will be conditioned by the vision you have for your company. The markets you enter, the technologies you choose, the performance you insist on achieving, the image you present to the world, the way you handle your people – all will depend on the end-point you have in mind. If your direction is unclear, your decisions will be muddled and your team in disarray.

But how do you know whether the course you've set is the right one? To answer that, you need lines of communication in almost every direction you can think of – down into your company, out into the markets, over into politics, technology and finance. You need people around you who can interpret accurately what is going on in each direction and what it implies for your strategy.

So you need to listen. And you need to select from what you hear. The knack of sorting good advice from bad, the under-standing of people involved in that judgement, are vital attributes in a leader.

Having formed your own vision, you must then, secondly, be able to communicate it. This book has looked at the ways it can be done. The absolute essentials are clarity and consistency. You must say what you mean, and mean what you say. And you must stick to it. And everyone must know that you will stick to it.

But you don't have to say very much. You never say anything publicly until you are sure of it. If you're not sure, you keep your silence. No leader is ever a blabbermouth. A leader speaks when he is sure.

As to the practical ability to realise your vision, that comes down to the management team you form around yourself. They are your strong right arm. Picking them, giving them clear goals, leaving them alone when necessary, lending a hand when necessary – these are the gifts of a leader.

And often there will be one person, perhaps two or three, with whom you are able to share your uncertainties in private. Such confidants, with whom you are totally frank and expect total frankness in return, can often provide new insights, helping you to be sure of your views before you make them public.

Leadership is always a lonely task. But no leader ever complains about that. He accepted the job because he wanted it. He therefore never asks for sympathy. But he does demand help, and he knows where to find it. My hope is that he will find some in this book.

Summary

· 30 ·

A Few Rules for the Road

Any chief executive who has read this book from end to end has given it a lot of his time. I thank him for his attention and hope he found it worthwhile. Every hour of his day is precious, I know, and much of the night. It is frightening how easily the plans you have made for your company can remain undone, lose momentum, gather dust. While others sleep untroubled you will often be up reading papers, checking figures, writing memos, dictating instructions, clawing back the hours lost to some interruption the day before. One thing I can say about you with complete certainty is that the moment you close this book, you will have a long list of other, more urgent things to think about.

So what parting message should you take from it?

Throughout I have tried not to lumber you with obvious reflections or facile advice. I have stuck to the job's essentials as I see them. Even so, a lot of ground has been covered – too much to be easily remembered in the rush of the onward journey. So are there a few common themes in what has been said? Can we find a few priorities that will form a manageable checklist?

I have six points to suggest. Three of them relate to the ways I think business will change in the 1990s; and three, I'd say, have always applied to the job of CEO.

First, then, the three which belong to our age:

- *Watch your market.* Very few markets will have static frontiers in the decade to come. We shall see more segmentation, more polarisation, more globalisation, more competition

from unexpected quarters, more virgin opportunities opening up. Whole new markets will appear; old markets will be
transformed or vanish altogether. So watch your own like a
hawk. Keep your eye on its edges and how they are moving.
Define precisely the segment you're aimed at and be sure to
keep your competitive advantage. Get this wrong, even
briefly, and you could be out of business.

- *Watch your technology.* Dramatic further changes in technology are coming, eclipsing anything seen so far. No market
  will be untouched by this; no company can ignore it. So be
  sure that your own technology is up to scratch. Assess it all
  the time against the latest developments, those that are just
  round the corner, and those on the far horizon. You can't
  afford to fall behind in the race, but misguided expenditure
  could ruin you. Make sure that you have all the advice you
  need to form the best possible judgement.

- *Watch your people.* The relationship between employer and
  employee is changing fast. By the year 2000 it will be very
  different. Good people are scarce and getting scarcer, and
  they know it. They expect more from their working life, and
  have the mobility to demand it – not simply better pay, but
  better conditions, better training, better prospects, a better
  environment. So make sure your own are satisfied. To
  recruit and keep good people, without which no success is
  possible, you must offer them more opportunity and reward
  than the competition.

Markets, technology, human resources: these, I think, will be
the prime sources of pressure in the 1990s, and between them
they could alter the nature and shape of your company. You
shouldn't be surprised if the end of the decade finds you or your
successor presiding over a business that is radically different
from today's.

All this fluidity, however, makes it more important than ever
to respect the rules of good management. These don't change
much from epoch to epoch, but three, I believe, deserve a place
on this final checklist.

- *Look for the angles.* Business today is such a complex art that easy answers to routine questions are not just a form of idleness: they're a dangerous trap. So poke around below the surface of the information and advice you are given. It's the mark of a good chief executive that he asks the awkward question, very often a simple question, which strips through the preconceptions and assumptions built into what he's being told. He's not easily satisfied; he keeps asking *why*, not from cussedness, but because he is searching for the true drivers of his company's performance and the essence of its competitive advantage.

- *Hold to your vision.* Despite, or perhaps because of, today's hectic pace of change, success most often goes to the company with a clear and consistent vision. Only you can provide this. It is a chief executive's business to set his company's course, to see that it's well understood by every employee, and to keep on driving the whole of the organisation towards that long-term goal.

- *Provide a clear lead.* Modern business favours flat command structures and participative decision-making, and there are good reasons for this. But don't try to manage by consensus. This has never worked, and never will. It is simply a cover for weakness in the chief executive. Time and again, this book has come back to the paramount importance of clear, firm leadership. There is no substitute for this. You can listen to other views, yes, but in the end it is you who must decide. That's what you are paid for.

With these six points, which I hope are not too preachy or personal, I will take my leave and let you get back to running your business. And my last word is to wish you luck. We all need a little bit of that.

Index

accounting 59–64
acquisitions 7, 21, 88–96, 126
administration 103
Allen, Woody 128
American market, the 13–14
Amstrad 18, 37, 38
analysts 59
Apple 18, 132
Apricot 14
atmosphere, company 121
auditors 59, 61

bankers 59
Benetton 68
Bhopal disaster 26
Black & Decker 17
Body Shop 26
Branson, Richard 93, 130
British Airways 71, 127–8
British Rail 109
British Telecom 14
brokers 59
budgeting 63
bureaucracy 60, 102

capital growth 92
career reviews 144
Carlzon, Jan 87
Carnaud 132
cash management 59, 60
cassette recorders 17
Castro, Fidel 83
Caterpillar Tractors 71
CBI 52
cellular telephones 17
chairman, the 134–9
challenge 3–5
change
    response to 23, 27
    vulnerability to 19
charts 140

Chernobyl disaster 26
City, the 60, 93, 113, 114
Clarks Shoes 47
clingfilm 17
clocks 70
collaboration, in research and development
    39–40
Coloroll 19
communication
    dangers of poor 92, 121
    internal 121–5, 137
    technology 7
    with customers 77
    with investors 111–15
    with media 6, 116–17, 137
    with shareholders 137
compact-disc players 39
competition, for business 7, 12, 19, 54
computers 18
Concorde 18
confidence 3
consensus management 70
consistency 129
corporate culture 15, 57, 126–9
corporate image 107, 117
cost assessments 25
cost
    of infrastructure
    of research and development 37–41
Court Lines 61
customer service 77, 151

Deming, Dr W Edwards 70
deregulation 20, 88, 151
Dewe Rogerson 114, 115
distribution 68, 91
diversification 19–22, 55
Dunlop 18

economic growth 70
employee suggestions 74, 123

empowerment, of employees 76
environmentalism 26–8
'Euromanagers' *see* management
Europe 64
exchange control authorities 59
Exxon Valdez 26, 109

fashion 19, 20, 21
fax machines 17
Federal Express 71
finance director 59–64, 136
financial
  engineering 60
  information 60–4
  institutions 60
  management *see* management
  reporting 60
focus 14, 15
Fokker-VFW 126
Ford, Henry 73, 122
forecasts 25, 62, 63
foresight 28
forward planning 60
Fuji Xerox 51

GEC 137
glass 23–4
Glaxo 25
globalisation
  of markets 6, 12, 148, 159
  of technology 44
government agencies 59
Grand Metropolitan 14
'green business' *see* environmentalism
growth 97–104
Guevara, Che 83

Hanson, Lord 60, 117
Harley-Davidson 71
Harvey-Jones, John 116
Hewlett-Packard 71
hi-fi 70
Hoare Govett 20
Horlicks 12
human resources 89, 151

IBM 18, 71, 116, 151
ICI 27, 46, 97, 149, 151
industrial relations 148
information 67, 73, 161
information technology 45–7, 64, 65, 67, 68, 89
Inland Revenue 59
integration, within the company 44
intrapreneurs 97–9
investor relations 111–17

Jaguar 71

JAL 98
John Lewis Partnership 150
Johnson & Johnson 33
J Walter Thompson 12

Keeler 33
Komatsu 74

lawyers 59
leadership 3, 124, 153–5, 161
legislation 27, 28
Linn Products 67
Lloyds Bank 20
Lloyd-Webber, Andrew 93
Lonrho 137

management
  burn-out 145
  cash 59, 60
  consensus 70
  control 55
  demotivated 142–6
  'Euromanagers' 147–9
  financial 58–64, 102
  mushroom theory of 123
  of change 85–7
  of high growth 97–104
  of research and development 41–4
  quality of 90
  rapid 68
  senior 74
  'Total Quality' 72–5, 127
manufacturing 8, 65–9
market
  new 19
  research 25
  understanding your 11–25
  watching your 159–60
'market focus' 16, 18
marketing
  career 11
  director, the 12
  test 25
Marshall, Colin 127–9
material rewards 4
Maxwell, Robert 115
McDonald's 12
Mercedes Benz 71
mergers 21, 88–96, 126
Metal Box 132
Midland Bank 24
mineral water 17
Moriya, Tohru 98
motivators, of chief executives 4
Murdoch, Rupert 70, 108

National Health Service 56
new product development 23–5

Nissan 148
non-executive directors 134–9

office politics 123, 140
Ovaltine 12

P&O 108
PA Consulting Group 12, 14, 26, 33, 35, 41, 43, 52, 61, 71, 75, 83, 84. 97, 99, 102, 108, 111, 116, 134, 148, 150
Parkinson, C Northcote 142
performance, of company
  analysis of 54–5
  commitment to 56–7
  improvement of 56, 65, 141
  measurement of 53–4
  significance of 51–2
Perrier 17, 109
personal checklist, for chief executives 52
personnel 84, 107
pharmaceutical industry 33, 39, 42
photocopiers 17, 70
pianos 70
Pilkington 23–4
pilot projects 25
Plastow, David 122
polarisation, of markets 7, 159
Polly Peck 58
press, the 116
pride in the job 4
Prince 18
Procter & Gamble 71, 77
product development 67
product maintenance 42
production 84
production engineering 66
production manager 67
productivity 51–2, 65, 71, 73
promotion 143, 150-52
psychometric testing 132, 143
public flotation 92
quality 70–7

'rapid response' 65–9
Really Useful Company 93
recruitment 35
research and development 32–44, 71
responsibilities, of chief executives 6
robotics 70
robots 68
Roddick, Anita 26
Rolls Royce 125

Saatchi & Saatchi 20, 94
sales 11, 141, 143
SAS 87
Security Pacific 20
segmentation of markets 159

semiconductors 70
shareholders 107
Shell 63
shipbuilding 70
short-termism 112–14
Sieff, Lord 124
Sinclair 18, 20, 37, 38
Single Market, the 147
Slazenger 18
Smith, Adam 73
Sony 18, 24, 31, 133
strategy
  analysis 81–2
  and research and development 41, 43–4
  business 89
  competitive 11
  corporate 7, 21, 41, 64, 89, 108
  formulation 82–3
  implementation 83–6
  operational 89
structures, within the company 142
Sugar, Alan 115
survey, into attitudes of chief executives 6–8, 11, 52, 111–15, 150, 154
sympathy 3, 134
synergy 21, 93–5

Tate & Lyle 137
taxation 60
team, choosing a 130–33
technical director 35
technological innovation 65
technology 7, 18, 19, 31–47, 52, 89, 91, 160
  see also information technology
Thorn EMI 137
time 46
'Total Quality' 65, 70–7, 127
Toyota 65–6, 68

Unilever 97, 152

Vickers 122, 137
video recorders 70
Virgin 93
vision 155, 161
Volkswagen 65
Volvo 73

watches 70
Weadlock, Daniel P 142
wealth-creation 4
Weinstock, Lord 60
Whitbreads 125

Yamaha 18
Young, John A 70

zips 70